MIRROR MOMENTS

Sharon Fletcher

Heather Bunch

Donna McDaniel

For more information on this book
or other encouraging resources, please visit

Gods-Best.com

Originally written in July 2019, printed in August 2019.

For ordering information, please contact admin@pwmin.org.

Special Thanks:

A heartfelt thank you goes to our wonderful editor Hannah Fletcher for poring over these words and making sure they made sense grammatically and stylistically! Her heart for excellence for God's glory shines through everything she does and there is no way we would have gotten all of this done on time without her diligence and effort! We love you Goose!

To Charleen Garrett for her wise eyes that helped us in the editing process as well. I am so excited for the next installment of *Mirror Moments for Grandmas* that you are going to write! And thank you for your prayers and encouragement. You are always a light that points to Jesus.

To my husband Greg Fletcher, who has laid out the copy and designed all of the covers and pages of all of our books. I had no idea how many amazing gifts God placed in you when we got married, but He has blown me away time and time again with you! I love you just doesn't seem like it's enough, but it's all I have. Thank you!

Sharon

About the Authors:

Sharon Fletcher

Sharon is a Texas-born woman of God who has a passion for Jesus and sharing His love with everyone who will listen. Together with her husband, Greg, she has co-authored several books and studies including Powerful Peace, Tools for Living, and Mirror Moments. Sharon also acts as a mentor for ladies who want to grow into their purpose and walk with Christ. She is a mother of 4 beautiful children and considers motherhood her highest calling, even above ministry.

Donna McDaniel

Donna grew up with the military lifestyle, graduated high school in Texas, graduated college in Kansas, met her husband in Seattle, Washington and grew in her faith in St. Louis, Missouri. Now she is a wife to Brian, mother and teacher to Cooper and Easton, and mentor to women. After writing *Oaks & Acorns: How to Mentor and be Mentored*, she had a life-change and moved from one state to another and began homeschooling her sons. She has called Sharon friend for 10 years and considers her and her husband, Greg, as the greatest influencers of her life through mentoring, and books they have written. Donna is honored to be a part of these devotionals and prays over each and every one of you who picks this book up. The Lord sees you and the Lord hears you. Love!

Heather Bunch

You know how when we were little girls, we had big dreams of a life full of purpose, an amazing career and the perfect little family? But, have you noticed many women discover that their dreams and reality don't match? Fear, poor self-image, and the hurts of life have held them back. Through coaching, writing and speaking, Heather Bunch helps women close the gap between their dreams and reality by uncovering who God created them to be so they can now enjoy a life of love, joy and legacy. Discover more at heatherlbunch.com.

Heather helped start Element Church in Wentzville, MO in 2005. Now, as the Wentzville campus Small Groups Pastor, she continues to be an integral part of helping them love God and love people.

She and her husband, Bob, are blessed with three miracle children. When not heading to the "Magic," aka Disney World, they love creating content for their YouTube channel so others can enjoy more magic too.

Introduction:

There is a spiritual principle at work in our lives. We will reproduce what we gaze at. The people or situations that capture our attention today influence what we will become tomorrow. As believers, we can learn to cooperate with this principle and engage with the Holy Spirit as He leads us into maturity.

In 2 Corinthians 3:18, Paul says, "But we all, with unveiled face, beholding as in a mirror the glory of the Lord, are being transformed into the same image from glory to glory, just as by the Spirit of the Lord." As we see God's character in God's Word for what it truly is, we grow in love for Him. As we see God's purpose for our lives, we joyfully submit to Him. As we see God's goodness, we worship Him. As we see Jesus for Who He is, we become like Him.

Spend a few moments gazing at the reflection of your Father and Your Lord today and let His Words inspire, heal, and encourage you!

I Am Defined by God Alone

*See how great a love
the Father has bestowed on us,
that we would be called children of God;
and such we are.
For this reason the world does not know us,
because it did not know Him.*

1 John 3:1 (NASB)

Looking at a fun-house mirror is entertaining at a carnival, but we would never try to use one to put on our makeup in the morning or fix our hair. The warped mirror will make one part of our body look distended and another part shrunken down. It distorts what is our true image and replaces it and emphasizes things that aren't really that important. The world's view of us tries to do that same thing in our lives—telling us that popularity with other people is of paramount importance, or that having a lavish lifestyle is the true indicator of success.

So, where do we go to find out who we are? Who really knows the truth about us? God does and God has called us His children.

Because we are His children, the world doesn't recognize what we are. We aren't part of the world's way of doing things and we don't fit into the mold people around us would try to put us in. If we are trying to find our identity in the vision others have of us, we will get it wrong. Every. Single. Time. The world just doesn't recognize what or who we are. It's not even able to.

Only God really knows who we are, even we don't fully recognize our new selves!

To see our true selves, we need to spend time with Him and His Word, seeing our reflection revealed in His face of love for us. Make the decision to find yourself in Him today! —SF

Day 2

I Am Beautiful

For You formed my innermost parts;
You knit me [together] in my mother's womb.
I will give thanks and praise to You,
for I am fearfully and wonderfully made;
Wonderful are Your works,
And my soul knows it very well.
My frame was not hidden from You,
When I was being formed in secret,
And intricately and skillfully formed
[as if embroidered with many colors]
in the depths of the earth.

Psalm 139:13 - 15 (AMP)

My two young girls adore dress up. One morning, they picked out particularly pretty dresses. After donning their outfits, my oldest girl admired herself in the mirror. Then proclaimed with enthusiasm, "I'm so beautiful!" This one sentence was said without shame, in full assurance that it was the truth. She then encouraged her little sister to join her, exclaiming, "look you're so beautiful!" Their delight in themselves was sweet and innocent.

How many of us adults look in the mirror each morning and say with enthusiasm, "I'm beautiful!"? Most of us are holding back the criticism or worse, declaring our criticism freely. We've been telling ourselves the negative aspects of ourselves for so long, we believe it.

Beauty is about loving who God created us to be. It's about seeing past the imperfections to our true selves–fearfully and wonderfully made. I'd like to propose an experiment. Look in the mirror and say to yourself, "who does my Creator see?" Then answer with only positive attributes. This helps you see yourself as He sees you. You're agreeing with Him! He intricately and skillfully formed you as if He was embroidering with many colors! He's continually thinking how amazing you are! —HB

Day 3

I Am Supplied

*Grace and peace be multiplied to you
in the knowledge of God and of Jesus our Lord;
seeing that His divine power has granted to us
everything pertaining to life and godliness,
through the true knowledge of Him
who called us by His own glory and excellence.*

2 Peter 1:2-3 (NASB)

So many times in life we feel inadequate to the tasks in front of us. We see the needs around us and look at our own resources or abilities to meet those needs and find quite a difference between them!

When my first child was born and I looked at his sweet, surprised face, I felt completely inadequate to the task of raising him. After a few days of diapers, nursing, and lack of sleep, I remember feeling like this was the longest babysitting job ever, and I wasn't a fan!

The good news for the Christian woman of God is that we aren't limited by our own resources, wisdom, or abilities. As I started to pray and ask God for help in raising up my son as unto the Lord, God started to reveal His power and grace to me. I started having His joy in my heart and truly enjoying loving my son with His love, serving my husband with His grace, and rejoicing in that season of my life.

God has promised us in His Word to be our source! The revelation that we don't have it all together is actually the beginning of victory in Jesus! When we know we don't have what it takes to win on our own, we will stop trying to rely on ourselves and instead pray and receive all that we need from God. 2 Peter 1 reminds us that HE grants us all we need for EVERYTHING pertaining to LIFE and GODLINESS through our knowledge of Him—our belief and reliance on God and what He has done for us through Christ.

Take some time right now to tell God where you don't have it all together and let Him fill your inadequacies with His all-sufficiency! -SF

Day 4

I Am Loved

For God so loved the world,
that He gave His only begotten Son,
that whoever believes in Him shall not perish,
but have eternal life.

John 3:16 (NASB)

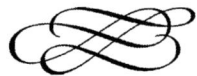

The Lord had been dealing with me for weeks before my 18th birthday. He was convicting me of living like a Christian on Sundays, but living like the world on Monday through Saturday. I hadn't even considered that I was supposed to be the same person at school that I was at church. Christianity had been a persona I put on to impress my friends or my parents' friends when I wanted to look like I had it all together. But it didn't really mean anything to me personally; I was simply playing the part of "a good Christian girl" when it suited my goals.

This all changed one night when the Holy Spirit convicted me of living like the world most of the time. He told me I needed to get on one side of the fence or the other. I contemplated giving everything I knew up and I realized the deepest desire in my heart was to be accepted and loved, so I cried out to Him, "Do you love me?" I knew that if He loved me, I could give up everything else that I used to try and fill that void—that deepest need in all of us for unconditional love.

His answer to me was to point to the cross. "Of course I love you! I sent my Son to die for you!" I had heard and believed that Jesus' death was for my sins, but I had never considered that it was an active expression of God's deep love for me personally. His answer still disarms me today as I ponder the significance of a Father willing to sacrifice His own, perfect Son for the rebellious, broken woman that I was. Jesus was God's love letter to me. Jesus is God's love letter to you, too. Everything He did was to demonstrate God's love for you. Every word He spoke was to illuminate God's will for you. He wants you to KNOW that He loves you and act on that knowledge by trusting Him in every area of your life.

Take some time right now to imagine what you would do if you KNEW that God loved you enough to send His Son for you personally. Then believe it! —SF

I Am Not Bound by My Past

Come, see a man,
which told me all things that ever I did:
is not this the Christ?

John 4:29 (KJV)

I was once drawn to share my first memories as a young girl, starting from grade school, to high school, and finally college, with a guy I was dating. I definitely do not encourage or recommend sharing all past sins in relationships, since God has made all things new and we are new creations in Him. Bringing up the past can lead to condemnation, especially when the partner isn't a Christian or is immature in their faith. With that said, his perspective of me changed. He now knew everything about me.

In Jewish tradition, women gathered together in the early morning to pull the day's needed water. This Samaritan woman chose the sixth hour, which is noon and the hottest part of the day, to separate herself from others and avoid her feelings of shame and embarrassment stemming from her life choices. Her conversation with Jesus brings us into an experience unheard of during these times—a Jewish rabbi speaking to a Samaritan woman! The Lord has love for each one of us! Despite our sin, we can be loved by the Lord! The Father knows everything about us, and because of Jesus, He sees spotless, blameless, and cleansed daughters of a King! His perspective of us has not changed, and despite knowing every single thing about us, He loves us.

That guy I was dating actually became my husband. Despite his new perspective of me, he loved me. I am not perfect. He realized he wasn't perfect either. We went into marriage seeking a perfect Savior who would take these two imperfect people and intertwine them into a three-fold cord.

Take some time to tell your Father in heaven all of your past. Let go of the afflictions you are holding on to and give it to the your Father! He wants you to be free of bondage and chains. These chains hold you down from knowing how much you are loved. Break free! He wants you to know that no matter how great you feel the mistakes may be, His son Jesus overcame them so that you may know the Father intimately! His perspective of you doesn't change! —DM

I Am Adored

*Husbands, love your wives,
just as Christ also loved the church
and gave Himself up for her,
so that He might sanctify her,
having cleansed her by the washing
of water with the word,
that He might present to Himself the church
in all her glory,
having no spot or wrinkle or any such thing;
but that she would be holy and blameless.*

Ephesians 5:25-27 (NASB)

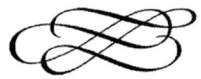

It is an amazing thing to consider that we are the Bride of Christ. The way that He sees us is full of love and adoration at the beauty God has given to us because of Christ.

My son recently got married in 2017, and he was so excited! He was visibly tearing up when He saw his bride, the love of his life, for the first time in her wedding attire. He had been dreaming of this day for months as they planned and prepared everything for the wedding celebration. It was made even more special because they had decided to wait until the ceremony for their first kiss.

Our Bridegroom Jesus is just as excited to see us face to face at His Second Coming! He longs to look into our eyes and profess His love for us in person, not just through the Holy Spirit and the Word of God. And because of His work on the Cross, we are made completely clean and righteous in His sight. We are beautiful! Song of Solomon is full of the beautiful imagery of a bridegroom speaking words of love and adoration to his bride that also apply to us in Christ. Those words of love were put in the Bible for us to understand the love of Jesus for us and to receive His deeply felt affection for us.

An amazing thing occurs once we receive this report. When we truly believed we are loved and accepted by Jesus, we start to act as though we are loved. We stop trying to fill this very real need with food. We stop looking for external approval by improving our appearance. We are satisfied with the looks of love from our Father and we no longer seek the validation of others for our existence. We KNOW we are deeply loved and our peace and joy overflows to all the areas of our lives.

Take a moment to reflect on how accepting this truth would radically change your behavior. Think about areas where you might feel unloved and let the love of God wash over you to heal and protect your heart. Choose right now to believe His love for you is real and true for YOU. It is! —SF

I Can Receive
If I Change
What I Believe

So Sarai said to Abram,
"Now behold, the Lord has prevented me
from bearing children.
Please go in to my maid;
perhaps I will obtain children through her."
And Abram listened to the voice of Sarai.

Genesis 16:2 (NASB)

God promised Abraham that he would be the father of many nations. Although he had no children of his own, God told him He would use his seed, his children, to bless the whole world. But after years of trying to conceive with his wife Sarah, things just weren't happening for him like he hoped. It's hard to imagine what was going through Sarah's mind when she presented her maid to her husband to "help" God's plan along. I believe she wanted to be a good wife, but had accepted the lie that because she was barren, she didn't have a part in God's plans to prosper Abraham.

There are many women in this same boat today that have painfully struggled with infertility for years to no avail. But honestly, we all struggle with fruitlessness in some area of our lives, whether it's with bearing children, having solid family relationships, a missed opportunity in our calling, a broken promise of fidelity, or a botched attempt at easing our own pain with drugs or alcohol. Sarah had misinterpreted her inability to have children as God's will for her. It is so very easy to look at our negative circumstances and wrongly identify them as God's will for us. It happens ALL THE TIME, and it can hinder the work of God in our lives.

Before Sarah was able to conceive her long-awaited and promised child —Isaac— she had to change this belief. As we see her wrestling with the idea that God DID want her to prosper in her body by bearing a child, she responded by incredulously laughing at the prospect (Genesis 18). She couldn't hardly believe this stranger prophesying to her that she would indeed bear a son who would go on to father the nation of Israel. As this truth became apparent in her heart over the next few months, she was finally able to conceive, and the desire of her and Abraham's hearts was gloriously filled with a bouncing baby boy!

Consider in your own life where you may have misinterpreted God's will for you because of negative circumstances or negative reports directed at you. Perhaps those in authority over you mislabeled you as a failure, a misfit, a reject, unusable by God. Perhaps you have even said and believed those things about yourself. Today, release those things to God and stop looking to the circumstances against you as being His will for you. The real truth is found in His Word, and it's only GOOD NEWS! —SF

Day 8

I Am Renewed Daily

Therefore we do not lose heart.
Though outwardly we are wasting away,
yet inwardly we are being renewed day by day.
For our light and momentary troubles
are achieving for us an eternal glory
that far outweighs them all.
So we fix our eyes not on what is seen,
but on what is unseen,
since what is seen is temporary,
but what is unseen is eternal.

2 Corinthians 4:16-18 (NIV)

I've been painting our new house with my mother-in-love for five days. She is going on 70, but looks 50. Every day I think she may text to say she cannot do another day, but she doesn't. See, we are hand-painting with 2-inch brushes a 3600-square-foot, textured-wall house. Why? Because that is the way she wanted to do it, and I'm not about to ridicule free help. We're going on the sixth day and she has already texted me, "A hot cup of chai tea, Tylenol, some Jesus, and the rest of a cookie and I'll be ready for tomorrow!" I'm in my thirties, and my body is crying, "Come back, Jesus, I'm ready!"

For her, she has fixed her eyes on the unseen. She knows she may not have much time left to be with us in this temporary world, but she gazes at the eternal glory. I've had conversations, that I've never had with anyone else, with her before, and her joy is bleeding through the paintbrush onto the freshly painted walls. And every day, she walks in with a fresh, renewed happiness unheard of on this earth.

The moment we are born, our bodies began a "grow and deteriorate" cycle of life. Our bodies are not made to last forever, but our souls are. When we realize that the only thing that matters is renewing daily in our Lord Jesus, we do not lose heart on the circumstances around us. We realize troubles are only momentary and we fix our eyes on the everlasting strength and victory we are given by our heavenly Father.

Take a minute, close your eyes. Pray for a daily inward renewal that overpowers any thoughts on outward renewal. Thank the Lord for hearing your prayer and giving you an eternal glory that outweighs any momentary trouble you may have. — DM

Day 9

_____

I Am Accepted

_Blessed be the God and Father of our Lord Jesus Christ,
who has blessed us with every spiritual blessing
in the heavenly places in Christ,
just as He chose us in Him
before the foundation of the world,
that we should be holy and without blame before Him,
in love having predestined us to adoption as sons
by Jesus Christ to Himself,
according to the good pleasure of His will,
to the praise of the glory of His grace,
by which He made us accepted in the Beloved._

Ephesians 1:3-6 (NKJV)

When Adam and Eve sinned in the Garden of Eden, they interrupted God's plans of blessing for them and their children. When Jesus purchased us back on the Cross, He brought us back into the blessings of God in such a way that it is no longer dependent on us to maintain that position or relationship. Jesus' righteousness was the final word on who we are now to God. He took our sinful and rebellious relationship with God and gave us His relationship with the Father instead, so that now no matter what we do, we are always accepted and beloved. This was His gift to us! God loves us so much! His plans for us are too great for us to comprehend in this lifetime. The mercy and grace He pours out on us through Christ will take an eternity for us to fully receive, but He wants us to start today!

During a very hard financial season for my husband and I in our early marriage, I was struggling to find money with which to buy groceries for our family. We had two young children at home at the time and payday was over a week away. I prayed and begged God for help and listened for His response. I poured out my needs and stretched my meager faith out to grasp the blessings of God that He promised to us in His Word.

For a few days, I kept getting an image in my spirit of a green CD holder we had. I just couldn't shake it. It was really weird, to be honest! Finally, I went and found it in my husband's nightstand and opened it. There was $100 in it! My husband had put the money in it a few months prior at a family Christmas gathering and had forgotten all about it. God's provision was there all along, but I had to ask, I had to listen, I had to believe, I had to respond in faith. That story is an example of all the blessings that are ours in Christ, but we haven't discovered yet. We may even have known some of these promises in the past, but forgot all that was included in our inheritance. Spend time now asking Him to meet your needs because of who you are in Christ! —SF

I Make God Happy

The Lord your God is with you,
the Mighty Warrior who saves.
He will take great delight in you;
in his love he will no longer rebuke you,
but will rejoice over you with singing.

Zephaniah 3:17 (NIV)

Have you ever considered that you actually make your Heavenly Father happy? Zephaniah even goes so far as to say He takes great delight in you! Now, if we were to say we took "great delight" in something, then that thing would be very important to us. I know I take delight in a really nice chocolate fudge, or a beautiful walk on the beach. But in my life, I reserve "great delight" for things like my wedding, the birth of my children or grandchildren, or maybe a long-awaited vacation to Ireland. So when God says He "takes great delight in you," He is trying to get across to us that He cares for us deeply and we make Him supremely happy! He is excited every time we enter His Presence in prayer. He longs for us to come and crawl into His lap and pour out our concerns to Him and surrender them to Him, knowing He is watching over us constantly.

If we need proof of this amazing level of affection, we have to look no further than the cross of Jesus Christ. We know that our current circumstances aren't an accurate reflection of Who God is, so we have to turn back to the cross—an unchanging monument to His character. God's love for us was on full display as He poured out the entirety of His righteous wrath from our sinful rebellion on His own Son. God didn't want us to have to taste any of it—not one single drop. That was the level of His love you us, for you!

Take some time right now to meditate on God's love for you and how much you make Him happy just because you allowed Him to save you! Say, " I make God happy!" and believe it! —SF

Day 11

I Am An Heir of God's Promises

And if you are Christ's,
then you are Abrahams' seed,
and heirs according to the promise.

Galatians 3:29 (NKJV)

In 2018, we watched on our television England's monarchy display a lavish, royal wedding for all the world to witness. This wedding laid out as if Cinderella herself planned each and every detail. As commoners though, we can only dream of a wedding that would turn the world's eye.

Unlike the heirs to England's or any other country's monarchy, our inheritance is rooted and unshakable by the world's instability. I love the Message version of Galatians 3:29: "In Christ's family there can be no division into Jew and non-Jew, slave and free, male and female. Among us you are all equal. That is, we are all in a common relationship with Jesus Christ. Also, since you are Christ's family, then you are Abraham's famous 'descendant,' heirs according to the covenant promises."

We don't have to dream of having a wedding that turns the world's eye, because right where we are, we get to be princesses in our own Cinderella love story! Our Lord and Savior takes us by the hand, lavishes us with blessings, and hands us a crown. The Word says our names are written on His hands and He has a name for each one of us. What a glorious thought!

Take time right this minute to seek the promises of God! Open your Bible or get online and search. These promises, each and every one, are for you as a believer in Christ. For you as a princess!! Thank the Lord for the wonderful inheritance He has provided for you! — DM

God Wants to Bless Me

But seek His kingdom,
and these things will be added to you.
Do not be afraid,
little flock, for your Father
has chosen gladly to give you the kingdom.

Luke 12:31-32 (NASB)

Yes, it's true. God really does want to shower you with His blessings! The Greek words translated as "chosen gladly" in verse 32 literally mean, "to be well pleased with, take pleasure in, to be favorably inclined towards one." This means God is well pleased and actually greatly enjoys blessing you. He thinks it's a great idea, and in reality it was His idea in the first place.

Consider what life must have been like for Adam and Eve in the Garden of Eden. Before sin entered into the world, it must have been wonderful. They had no hard labor to accomplish with toil and tears. They had no pains and sorrows. They didn't even know what death was. All of Creation rejoiced in the Creator together, making a wonderful symphony—each instrument praising God in its own, unique way. This was God's original plan for you and me as well. And to be honest, His plans for you haven't really changed!

When Jesus reassured His disciples in Luke 12, He must have known that this idea is foreign to our natural minds. Our sinful, broken way of thinking reinforces to us the idea that if we aren't perfect in every way, we won't receive God's blessings because we don't deserve them. This was the entire reason for the coming of Jesus! He made us worthy and blessed when He gave us His righteousness and took our sinfulness on the Cross. This exchange was even God the Father's idea in the first place! That's how much He loves you!

Meditate on and confess this today: God has chosen gladly to give me the kingdom! Hallelujah! —SF

No Enemy Can Touch Me

*My sheep hear My voice,
and I know them, and they follow Me;
and I give eternal life to them,
and they will never perish;
and no one will snatch them out of My hand.
My Father, who has given them to Me,
is greater than all;
and no one is able to snatch them
out of the Father's hand.
I and the Father are one.*

John 10:27-30 (NASB)

There are times in our lives where we feel vulnerable and unguarded. A shocking development with a close relative, a negative report from a doctor, or an unexpected death of a friend can leave us feeling rattled and alarmed. Jesus knew these things could cause us to question the protection and love of our Father in Heaven. He reminds us here in John 10 that even though challenges come during our lives here on earth, we can trust that God and Jesus are both carrying us and holding us close.

We have a very real enemy on this earth, Satan, but fortunately for us, our big brother Jesus has already beaten him up severely when He resurrected! We never need to fear what the devil whispers to us in times of crisis. He can't actually do anything to us because we are in the protective Hands of our Father God, Who is greater than all! Try as he might, the devil can't snatch us away from our Father either! So if you are in the midst of a serious challenge in your life, lean into His bosom and rest. Let Him love you through it, and know that no one can snatch you out of His powerful hands!

Thank God for His sweet Presence in your life, even in the midst of struggle and fears, and know that He will never leave you nor forsake you! —SF

God Is Always With Me

My sheep hear My voice,
and I know them, and they follow Me;
and I give eternal life to them,
and they will never perish;
and no one will snatch them out of My hand.
My Father, who has given them to Me,
is greater than all;
and no one is able to snatch them
out of the Father's hand.
I and the Father are one.

John 10:27-30 (NASB)

Sheep tend to be very skittish creatures, and honestly, sometimes not very bright! They can get stuck in the silliest of places and are often unwise on where they choose to feed. When Jesus compares us—His disciples—to sheep, I think He knew we could often be guilty of the same foolishness! It's a wonder and a blessing that Jesus is such a good shepherd to us. Even when we wander off, seemingly on our own, His Presence is always only a whisper away. Honestly, He is as close to us as our breath. The word "spirit" in the New Testament is the word "*pneuma*" in Greek, which can also be translated as "breath." When we become born again, we receive God's "breath" in our hearts and spirits just like Adam received God's breath and became a living soul in Genesis 2:7. This Presence never leaves us; it is a gift that we didn't earn, so we can't lose. The only qualification we need is that we confess that Jesus—the Son of God— is our Lord and receive His sacrifice on the Cross and His resurrection as payment for all of our sins. Once we have done that, our salvation is eternal and secure!

We need to understand and believe that God actually wants to be with us forever. As a loving father Who wants to be actively involved in the daily lives of His children, our Father wants to inundate us with His love, wisdom, and blessings in every area of our lives, and because of Jesus He now has the right to do it! Meditate today on His great love for you and how happy He is now that He can spend every moment of your life with you! He is your Good Shepherd and is watchfully caring over your every step. —SF

I Am Content

*Make sure that your character
is free from the love of money,
being content with what you have;
for He Himself has said,
"I will never desert you,
nor will I ever forsake you,"*

Hebrews 13:5 (NASB)

Much of our discontentment and emotional turmoil stems from what we are meditating on and thinking about. When we are consumed with all of our challenges, or the circumstances we can't change, we are missing the true source of joy and happiness in our lives. When we believe our problems will be solved with more money, we become consumed with trying to meet our needs on our own. We start to fret and worry because we have forgotten that He is our source and joy and that He will take wonderful care of us if we let Him.

Even when we are going through hard seasons in our lives, we can be happily content because we believe He loves us and that He is working all things out according to His good and pleasant will for us. If we wait until all of our circumstances are "perfect" to be happy, we will never be happy. But when we can choose to be happy because He loves us, He will never leave us, and He is walking so closely with us every day, we can be truly happy in His Presence always. Honestly, if we have to have something other than His Presence to make us truly happy, we won't ever be truly happy. Such happiness doesn't exist.

C.S. Lewis wrote, "God cannot give us a happiness and peace apart from Himself, because it is not there. There is no such thing." [1]

Take a moment to rest your heart and mind on His love for you, knowing that in His Presence is the fullness of your joy! (Ps. 16:11)-SF

I Drop The Hot Thoughts

When angry, do not sin;
do not ever let your wrath
(your exasperation, your fury or indignation)
last until the sun goes down.

Ephesians 4:26 (AMPC)

Have you ever had a server at a restaurant warn you your plate is really hot so that you'll avoid touching it and getting burned? Or, have you ever touched the hot handle of a skillet on the stove? You immediately jerked your hand away, right? I promise this is not kitchen safety 101.

In your thought life, you may do the opposite. You'll "touch" or experience an unproductive or "hot thought," but then refuse to let it go. Sometimes, you might even pick up the hot thought over and over again, even though you know it's not helpful. Like the time your husband bought that big-ticket item when he knew that money was earmarked for something else. Or, the instance your friend said something hurtful about you behind your back. You mulled it over and over in your mind and couldn't put it down.

What did that hot thought produce? Nothing good. It just fueled negative thoughts and emotions. It brought you no joy. There is a better way. You can drop the hot thought.

Some people think they have to vent their frustrations, then they can "let it go." They may even feel it's their right to vent it. Is venting a prerequisite to dropping the thought? What if you could break the link at the beginning? If you're going to drop the thought eventually, why not drop it immediately?

By catching negativity early, you keep yourself in a resourceful state of mind, giving yourself the best shot at effectively solving problems, dealing with stress, overcoming challenges, and generating more joy.

Schedule a time with God to deal with your hot thought. Then, you can drop it knowing you can deal with it later in a more productive frame of mind. When the scheduled time comes to deal with that thought, you may find it's taken care of itself. But if not, you'll be able to handle it in a more godly manner now that the hotness has worn off. —HB

Day 17

I Am a Child of God

*For you have not received a spirit of slavery
leading to fear again,
but you have received a spirit of adoption
as sons by which we cry out,
"Abba! Father!"*

Romans 8:15 (NASB)

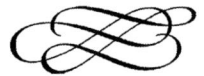

In the legal system in the United States, an adopted child has the same right as a natural-born child to the parents' inheritance and support. In Roman times, adoption was actually even more secure than being natural-born to the Roman parents. A natural-born child could be rejected by the father and "disowned" at birth but an adopted child was more secure than that, and chosen on purpose to fully be a part of the father's family. This child was able to not only permanently receive all the rights and privileges of any accepted and natural-born children, but also be a full joint-heir of the inheritance. It is God's intention to have this same relationship with us!

Some friends of mine adopted a son a few years ago. When they were fostering this young boy, and even in the early adoption period, the young boy struggled to believe that this was a permanent arrangement. He kept wondering if he would be rejected if he messed up, so he would try and hide any indiscretions and would be visibly upset when he was found out. Over time and repetition, he began learning that his new identity as an adopted son couldn't be changed by his own negative behaviors. This couple poured out the grace of God to this young, broken child and the amazing process of healing began.

Sometimes we struggle with this same attitude when it comes to our Father in Heaven. When we mess up, we may try to hide it from Him, or defend ourself vehemently all the while fearing that His love for us is somehow diminished because of our sin. Let me reassure you that this is not the case. Your relationship with the Father is so valuable to Him that He rejected and punished His Son on the cross in your place, so He would never have to reject you because of your sin! Yes, God disciplines us when we need it, just like any good parent would. But our relationship with Him is never in jeopardy, and all of His discipline is for our benefit. Come to Him freely today, taking any challenges you struggle with to Him. You will find Him the gracious, loving Heavenly Father—full of compassion and grace—that you secretly hope Him to be. —SF

Day 18

I Am Forgiven

Straightening up, Jesus said to her,
"Woman, where are they? Did no one condemn you?
She said, "No one, Lord.
And Jesus said, I do not condemn you, either.
Go. From now on sin no more.

John 8:10-11 (NASB)

A sinful, law-breaking, and adulterous woman was brought before Jesus. Her repugnant life brought a "we can trap Jesus" taste to the Pharisee's lips. But, does this trap go the way the rule-following, judgmental, and law-condemning ridiculers want?

I was 23 when a revelation spread over me like a fire consuming a thin sheet of paper. I was at small group Bible study watching a video about God wanting you to lay your past sins on Him. Driving home afterwards, I had to pull over. All the baggage I had been carrying all my life wasn't mine to carry any longer. God wanted it! He wanted me to lay my past, my shame, all the memories that were binding me to an old life separated from my heavenly Father, down.

I spent so much time condemning myself. I felt as though the "church-people" were condemning me too. I hid and put on a facade so they would like me. But the Lord said to me, "No. You are to become someone new, and now is the time to let the old go." The next time we were all together, through a tear-soaked face, I shared who I used to be. And wouldn't you know, several of my friends had similar stories. They knew the struggle and were free because of Jesus too!

I pray the woman who was brought to Jesus in John 8 felt the same freedom I did. We are not given an explanation of her feelings, words of gratitude, or even if her tears of joy caused a puddle at Jesus's feet. Jesus simply says, "I do not condemn you, either."

Take time right now to release the baggage that has followed you around chained to your ankle! You are free!! The Lord wants you to tell Him everything, and for you to know you are not alone!! — DM

Day 19

_____

I Am Amply Supplied

And my God will supply all your needs
according to His riches in glory in Christ Jesus.

Philippians 4:19 (NASB)

Many times, as believers, we struggle with the idea that God wants to bless us. We have been taught that God wants to give us poverty, sickness, or oppression to teach us holiness and humility. When we hold these ideas up to Biblical truth, however, they quickly wither up and fade away.

Let's consider what God's idea of "very good" is in light of His creation—the Garden of Eden. There were all sorts of fresh fruits of various types for Adam and Eve to pick from freely, and enjoy anytime they were hungry. There was no painful labor, no toil, not even any significant change in climate within the garden. They never got too cold, too hungry, too hot, or too tired. They simply basked in the wonderful provisions of their loving Heavenly Father and enjoyed wonderful fellowship with Him and one another. Because there was no sin, there were no strife-filled relationships or damaged emotional scars to deal with. They were happy and at peace, knowing the love of the Father at all times.

When sin entered into the equation, they were forced to leave this idyllic garden and enter the broken system of sin and death purchased with their disobedience. In order to get us back into the "very good" God had planned, He sent a sacrifice—Jesus Christ! Now, because of what Jesus did, we get the opportunity to enter that wonderful state of provision that Adam forfeited in the Garden. Hallelujah!

Take some time to imagine what your life would look like with the full goodness of God manifesting in your life right now, right here. Because of Jesus, that is yours! Thank God for His goodness and receive it by faith. —SF

Day 20

I Am Important to God

He who did not spare his own Son,
but gave him up for us all—
how will he not also, along with him,
graciously give us all things?

Romans 8:32 (NIV)

Little daughter of God, you have been told many times by the world that you don't matter. It's been said to you in word or action that you aren't worthy. You have heard that you are defective and don't quite measure up. You have thought that perhaps God can't love you because you are just too broken, too damaged, too defective to be any good.

The Creator of life, land, and sea knows everything there is to know. God knows the truth and He says something completely different about you. He says you are eternally loved and accepted and incredibly priceless—worth giving up His only Son for! He paid the ultimate price to see you set free from these lies and restored to a right relationship to Him. He chose to redeem you so He could overwhelm you with His love and overcome you with His providing grace. Jesus' death on the cross was His idea in the first place. He saw you right where you are and said, "That one! She is worth dying for!"

Knowing and believing such love and acceptance of the only One who truly knows us is life changing. And knowing that He paid such a high price for us will also change our prayer life. If we know He didn't spare His only Son, the most precious thing in creation to Him, we can't possibly believe He could withhold anything else of lesser value. Finances, health, peace, safety—all of these things pale in comparison to the matchless value of Jesus Christ Himself! If God didn't spare His own Son, it would be unimaginable for Him to deny us anything else.

Take this knowledge with you to the throne room as you pray for what you need right now! God didn't spare Jesus for you, so He won't deny you what you need. —SF

I Glorify God with My Life

Now to him who is able to do immeasurably more than all we ask or imagine, according to his power that is at work within us, to him be glory in the church and in Christ Jesus throughout all generations, for ever and ever!

Ephesians 3:20 (NIV)

It glorifies God to display His power in blessings upon your life! When His bride—the church—flows in the goodness of God, we reflect His character of love and blessing to those around us. The devil is running around all over this world today whispering in humanity's ear that God is an angry judge, just waiting for them to mess up so He can punish them, or that a good God doesn't even exist and that they are on their own. Our job as the body of Christ is to show Who God really is to the world. When we flow with the love of God to the people He places in our lives, they are blessed and God is glorified.

God's power flows through us in many different ways. Yes, we can help others financially, but it is much more than just that. We can flow in praying and laying on of hands for healing. We can speak life into the lives of those around us. We can offer a smile and a hug to those feeling unloved. We can serve the homeless, orphan, and widow. As long as we are listening and obeying the Holy Spirit's love within us, we will glorify Him naturally with our words, attitudes, and actions.

We can't discount the power of asking in prayer. The entire passage above starts with the idea that He is able to do immeasurably more than all we ask or imagine! That's a lot!

Take a few moments this morning to apply that faith and understanding of God's will to bless others around you. Pray for yourself, your family, your friends, your enemies, your leaders, and anyone else who comes to your mind, knowing and believing that God wants to bless them through you! —SF

Day 22

I Choose Productive Thoughts

The mind governed by the flesh is death,
but the mind governed by the Spirit
is life and peace.

Romans 8:6 (NIV)

There are no neutral thoughts. Each thought we think is either moving us closer to who God created us to be or further away. It's either serving us or not. It's either producing joy in our lives or not. One of the best ways I've found to choose productive thoughts is to ask yourself great questions. Great questions will produce great answers. Bad questions, well, they produce bad, unproductive answers. When you ask yourself a question, your mind goes to work automatically to find the answer. Bad questions, like, "why does this always happen to me," only extract an unproductive thought that doesn't help you get the solution you want.

Here are 5 questions that changed my life. These questions extract a positive response–the truth that God says about you. Try asking these questions daily for the next month to form the habit of asking great questions to produce positive thoughts. Miss a day? No worries, pick it up again the next day.

1. What 5 things am I thankful for right now? Past or present. Big or small.
2. What are 5 of my strengths or positive qualities? You know your weaknesses, but does it help if you focus solely on that? It's more valuable to focus on your strengths and positive qualities and develop those.
3. What are 5 of my greatest achievements so far? Again, this could be big or seemingly small.
4. Who are the 5 people who love me the most? Rather than thinking about the people who hurt you, who are the people who are there for you? Who are the people who love you enough to challenge you to be better?
5. What 5 things am I looking forward to in the next 7 days? Forecasting your future can bring you out of the present and help you look forward to what's ahead. There's always something to look forward to, even if it's just a payday, a birthday party or a beautiful sunrise. —HB

Day 23

I Abound in Every Good Work

And God is able to make all grace abound to you,
so that having all sufficiency in all things at all times,
you may abound in every good work.

2 Corinthians 9:8 (ESV)

When my husband and I were newly married, we had a very tight budget. I believe we had about $75 per week for groceries and eating out. I paid attention to every can of beans and every package of ground beef to make sure I had enough money to cover everything as I would stand in the check-out line. Many times I would have to put something back if I hadn't calculated correctly. How embarrassing it seemed at the time!

By God's grace and wisdom our finances improved, we were able to splurge a little more and my tight grip on my calculator thankfully loosened a little bit! Now, many years later, I am blessed to be able to walk through the grocery store without really giving the prices a second thought. I know our grocery budget is over and above anything we may need for the week, so I don't worry about it at all.

That is the image Paul is painting for us here in 2 Corinthians 9. He is trying to paint the vision for us that God is so supernaturally able to cause us to prosper in every way, that anything He calls us to do is no problem whatsoever. All we need in order to raise our families in Jesus, provide for all of our needs, and walk through this life with victory in every area, is provided richly for us so that we can abound in every good work! "Abounding" is such a rich word—it evokes the image of abundance, doesn't it? That is exactly what God wants for you in your everyday life. Lean in to His good character, wisdom, love, and grace for you today. You will find His supply for your every need to be over and above all you can ask or think! —SF

I Am Unique

*For we are His workmanship
[His own master work, a work of art],
created in Christ Jesus [reborn from above—
spiritually transformed, renewed,
ready to be used] for good works,
which God prepared [for us] beforehand
[taking paths which He set],
so that we would walk in them
[living the good life which He prearranged
and made ready for us].*

Ephesians 2:10 (AMP)

One area the devil likes to trap us is comparison with others. Our culture, and maybe even our friends, will hold up a pattern of what we should look like, what job we should have, or what our significant other should look like. Society provides an unrealistic image of success for us to emulate, and we feel like failures when we don't measure up. The problem with all of that is those patterns aren't the pattern God used when He created us.

I learned how to sew when I was in high school. One of the first things I learned was that I had to find the correct pattern to use to get the image of what I wanted to create right. If the wrong pattern had been put in the packaging, the pattern wouldn't produce the picture on the front of the package! Only God knows what the picture on our pattern looks like. God made each of us to be a different creation even before we were born. He had a special design for you and the pattern He placed in you is completely unique and special to the purpose He created you for. When we start comparing ourselves to other people, we aren't being fair to ourselves. God doesn't want you to look like everybody else. He created you uniquely special! God designed each of us differently on purpose, and comparing ourselves to one another and trying to be alike actually thwarts the plan of God for us. Our uniqueness is part of God's purpose in our lives. Let's celebrate our differences and the uniqueness of others!

Thank God today for the gifts and talents He has placed in you and decide today to quit comparing yourself to anyone else. God made you unique on purpose. You don't make a very good them, and they don't make a very good you either! —SF

I Am Dead to Sin

For the death that He died,
He died to sin once for all;
but the life that He lives, He lives to God.
Even so consider yourselves to be dead to sin,
but alive to God in Christ Jesus.

Romans 6:10-11 (NASB)

We were born in sin and it owned us. Honestly, we couldn't resist every temptation to begin with because the sin nature was part of who we were when we were born. It was passed on to us from our parents and grandparents who ultimately received it from Adam and Eve. We were slaves to it!

Now, because of Jesus we are set free! God allowed Jesus' death to sin to be transferred to us, so that the freedom He walked in on this earth now belongs to us! As Jesus walked around free from jealousies, striving, lying, fears, lusts, hate, outbursts of anger, and all the other things we struggle with daily, so can we. Our part in this transaction is to accept what Jesus did and consider it to be true for us. That's what faith is—accepting what God says about us as the truth. So now when we are presented with a temptation to be angry, lustful, jealous, or any other sin, we get to remember that we aren't a slave to those things any more. We have the life of Jesus Christ flowing through us and His freedom is now our freedom. His death to sin was our death to sin and our life is now completely hidden in Him!

As you go about your day today, and you are tempted to do the old familiar sins you have struggled with in the past, say this: I am dead to sin, it no longer controls me. I am now alive to God in Christ Jesus and I have His desires and walk in His righteousness! —SF

Day 26

I Am Well Watered

Seek the Lord and His strength;
Seek His face continually.

1 Chronicles 16:11 (NASB)

In 2019, Tulsa had torrential rain, flash flooding, tornados, and some of the most extreme weather they had in decades. But despite the crazy weather, our outside plants were growing incredibly and blooming beautifully. The amount of water led to this growth. After the many days of rain, I did not find it necessary to water the plants. Even several days after the rain, I still did not water the plants. They were fine, or so I thought.

Sometimes, we may find ourselves flooded with the Word of God! We can get inundated with church-serving opportunities and sharing Jesus with all whom we come in contact with. We can do Bible studies, speak to groups of people, and lead worship. We can essentially be "flash-flooded" by the incredible Good News of our Savior, Heavenly Father, and Holy Spirit! What a place to be!

But we are fleshly beings, and soon find that the flash flood recedes. What is left afterwards? We are like my plants in the backyard, already yearning for water again. They are actually drier than they were before the rains came. Why didn't that amount of water stay with them? I definitely have no degree in botany, nor know much more about plants than what my amazing sister-in-law has shared with me, but one thing I do know: they will quickly die if I don't keep them damp.

See, the flooding gave the plants lots of water all at once, but they were incapable of holding all of it. They need daily "dampening" from their owner. We, too, need daily dampening from our Savior, the one who has the Living Water. So how will you take in the Living Water daily? Create a plan for yourself right now! And follow it! —DM

Day 27

I Am A Lover

Beloved, let us love one another,
for love is from God,
and whoever loves
has been born of God and knows God.
Anyone who does not love does not know God,
because God is love.

1 John 4:7-8 (ESV)

As we are growing in our ability to reflect His character correctly, our love for one another will grow too! The part of us that is born of God—our spirit—will naturally respond to those around us with the love of God. As we mature in our walk with Christ, we will recognize His opinions of others and we will adopt that for ourselves as loving children desiring to adopt the attitudes and actions of their Father.

In 1 John 4, the apostle John is encouraging us to allow this love to flow through us to others. We don't have to strive for this to happen, we only have to agree with what God has already done for us in Christ. Jesus has taken the work of our sanctification upon Himself since we are unable to do it ourselves. And our job becomes allowing Him to do this work in our lives and hearts as we spend time in His Presence. As we do this, we are fulfilled and naturally reflect His goodness and loving character. When we see Jesus, what He has done for us, and how much He loves us, we can't help but be changed.

It reminds me of the cliché "to know me is to love me," but in this case it is actually true. To see and know God through Jesus Christ is to be enraptured with His glory and lost in His love for you.

Meditate on His deep and abiding love for you today and allow that love to flow through you to the lives in your path today! —SF

Day 28

I Am Forgiven

Therefore, my friends,
I want you to know that through Jesus
the forgiveness of sins is proclaimed to you.

Acts 13:38 (NIV)

Every person on this planet who has tried to pray to God is aware of their own inadequacy and sinfulness. In every country, every religion, there is some tenet that addresses the sin-consciousness we all find within ourselves. Buddhism teaches the idea of karma—your actions against natural law will come back to punish you at some point. Islam teaches that there can be forgiveness of minor sins if no major sins are committed, and that more good actions than bad will negate the bad. There is an innate sense of our value based on our behavior. No one has to tell us, our conscience just knows we have messed up our lives and hurt other people in the process.

The Holy Spirit works with this knowledge to bring us to see our need of redemption and forgiveness. Here, in his sermon in the book of Acts, Paul shares the wonder of God's plan for our redemption—forgiveness through the shed blood of another. All of us, sinners in the highest degree, were convicted of highest treason before God and sentenced to physical death and eternal separation from the Holy God we rejected. But Jesus stepped in and became our complete and total forgiveness, our "get out of hell free" card by substituting His own life for ours.

This news is so good that Paul felt the need to proclaim it! He preached it! He shared it! He lived it! Once this forgiveness gets into our hearts and minds and completely takes over, we do the same. We love, we forgive, we share, we proclaim, we broadcast the love and peace we have through Jesus to the broken and condemned world around us.

Meditate on your forgiveness today and all that God has paid for so you could be free! —SF

I Believe God's Promises

For when God made the promise to Abraham,
since He could swear by no one greater,
He swore by Himself, saying,
"I will surely bless you and I will surely multiply you."
And so, having patiently waited,
he obtained the promise.

Hebrews 6:13-15 (NASB)

We can always trust God when He promises something to us. He is incapable of not keeping His word. We WILL obtain the promises if we patiently wait. So where can we find these promises? In His Word. 1 Corinthians 1:20 tells us that all of God's promises are yes and Amen in Jesus Christ! This means that the promises were God's idea in the first place, and that Jesus' sacrifice makes us qualified to receive all of them because of His righteousness.

In order to agree with God's promises for ourselves, we have to understand that every promise is a reflection of the goodness of God's character and His desires for us. When we see how God promised to bring the Israelites out of bondage and into the Promised Land, we need to understand that it is a reflection of His desire for all of His people to live free of bondage and in overwhelming abundance. This desire isn't just for the children of Abraham, Isaac, and Jacob, but every one of us as well. Now, we may not be Egyptian slaves like the Jewish people once were, but we may be a slave to something else God wants to free us from. Every promise in the Old Testament reveals a facet of God's character, and illuminates part of His love for us and His good plans for us. He hasn't changed in His character. He is the same yesterday, today, and forever (Hebrews 13:8), so those promises for freedom, blessing, safety, health, and peace are the same for us today. How it manifests might be different because we live in a different time, but His desire to bless us is the same!

Pick one or two promises from the Old Testament that apply to you today because you are in Christ! —SF

I Choose Lovely Thoughts

*Finally, brothers and sisters,
whatever is true, whatever is noble,
whatever is right, whatever is pure,
whatever is lovely, whatever is admirable —
if anything is excellent or praiseworthy —
think about such things.*

Philippians 4:8 (NIV)

Would you like more joy in your life? We all want more joy.
God wants joy for us. He's created us for it. Children laugh an
average of 300 times a day. But, did you know, the average adult
typically laugh only 17 times per day? What happened between
childhood and adulthood? For most of us, a lot of challenges.
It's so easy to get caught up in challenges of life and forget what's
going right.

There will always be some unlovely junk in your life that you
could choose to dwell on, but that will not produce a joy-filled life.
It will produce a life of fear, hurt, anger, rejection, or defeat.
When you focus on the loveliness of your life, you'll not only
notice more loveliness, you'll create more of it. Choose to think
about what could go right instead of what might go wrong.

"He is a wise man who does not grieve for the things which he
has not, but rejoices for those which he has." - Epictetus

It's time to see the blessings that surround us. On one side of a 3x5
card write "increase." On the other side write "decrease."
Now write 3 lovely thoughts on the front that you want to
increase thinking about. On the back write 3 unlovely thoughts in
your life that you want to decrease thinking about. Put a giant X
through the unlovely thoughts. Now, keep this card with you so
you see it multiple times a day. When the unlovely thoughts come,
stop, and choose to think the lovely thoughts rather than dwelling
on the unlovely thoughts.

Why do this? Because you can't think one thing and expect to
experience something completely different. This is an act of
choice–a power that God gave you. You're not a victim of your
thoughts. Joy is a state of mind that must be cultivated. —HB

I Receive God's Word

*"Therefore, putting aside all filthiness
and all that remains of wickedness,
in humility receive the word implanted,
which is able to save your souls."*

James 1:21 (NASB)

This Scripture used to confuse me, because I thought Jesus saved our souls once and for all on the cross and that when we received it, we were saved. That is true, but that one time act of salvation is not exactly what James is talking about here in James 1. Let's do a little digging into the Greek language so we can get a better understanding about what he is saying to us.

The Greek word for "save" is "sozo" (soh-dzoh) and it means to protect, heal, restore, and return to original and pristine condition. When we are born-again, our spirit is instantly transformed into a new creature in Christ, but that's not the only part of us that needed redemption. We also have a soul—a mind, will, and emotions. In addition to redeeming our spirits, God wants to transform the way we think and reason in this life. He wants our souls to reflect His righteousness, His way of doing and being right. He wants our thoughts to agree with His whenever we encounter challenges and trials. He isn't ever worried or fearful when things don't go the way we think they should. He knows His power is more than enough to cause us to triumph in every situation, and He wants us to believe that too, and act like it!

If we want our minds to think correctly, our wills to function properly, and our emotions to be healthy, we have to receive God's Word into our hearts—to accept His Word as the truth, believing God is more than able to do all He has said He will do. This happens every day as we read God's Word and meditate on what He says is true. We have the freedom to meditate on whatever we want to, but only meditation on God's Word will change our souls into the image of Jesus! When we receive His Word, it changes and restores us. Receive His report about you today! —SF

I Fulfill God's Purpose in My Lifetime

For David, after he had served the purpose of God
in his own generation, fell asleep,
and was laid among his fathers
and underwent decay;.

Acts 13:36 (NASB)

One thing I just love about God and His Word is the fact that the only perfect person in the Bible is God Himself. Every other person mentioned in the Bible was full of weaknesses and fears. It actually brings me such hope to see how Abraham lied about his wife, calling her his sister, to avoid being bullied by the king of Egypt; or how Gideon was so fearful of the Philistines and was so unsure about God's protection that he had to make his meals in the middle of a grain silo to remain undetected—even after an angel of God appeared to him, he had a hard time believing the testimony of God for his life. And even Moses argued with God so much at the burning bush that he actually made God mad at him! Then there was Deborah, who complained against Moses and ended up bearing leprosy for awhile. And to top it all off, there is King David—the man after God's own heart—who committed adultery with the wife of Uriah, and then had Uriah killed when his wife turned up pregnant by David! Every single person mentioned in the Bible, from Adam to Paul and the other apostles, was riddled with doubts, fears, and sin. But God was able to use them for His glory anyway. As a matter of fact, it seems like God delights in using the weak things of the world to confound the wise. He is so sure of the power of His grace in our lives, that He can pick the weakest and saddest among us to showcase His goodness and faithfulness.

So let's not limit what God can do through us today because of our inadequacies. Our weaknesses don't discount us in His eyes. Our sins don't overcome His grace, but His grace overcomes our infirmities, and even reveals His goodness in our lives. Thank God that He can use you today for His purpose in your lifetime! -SF

I Am Valuable

*But you are a chosen generation, a royal priesthood, a
holy nation, His own special people,
that you may proclaim the praises of Him
who called you out of darkness into His marvelous light.*

1 Peter 2:9 (NKJV)

Have you ever thought someone else had more value than you? Have you thought that if you could do or be more, that would make you more valuable?

It was the 1950's in Thailand, and a group of monks discovered a clay statue was cracked. After chiseling off the layers of clay, they revealed a solid gold statue underneath worth 197 million dollars. It was hidden beneath layers of clay for decades. No one could see its true value.

You might say to yourself, "I'm broken," or "what's wrong with me." You might think others are more valuable. But, you're like the golden statue covered in layers of clay. Over the years, layers of crud have developed over you from fears, challenges, rejections, hurts, and wrong thinking.

But, your true self is more valuable than you think. God said He knit you together in your mother's womb. He said you're fearfully and wonderfully made, you're a new creation in Christ, you're a chosen generation, you're a royal priesthood, and you're the righteousness of God in Christ Jesus. You're so valuable that Jesus gave His own life for you! Not because He needed another servant, but because He loves you and wanted to be your friend (John 15:15).

How do you chisel away the layers of crud hiding your true self? By choosing true thoughts and believing the correct story about yourself. Remind yourself what your Heavenly Father says about you. As you do this, your real self is revealed and you can see your true value: priceless.

Take a few minutes siting in God's presence. Ask Him to show you how valuable you are. Write down every great thing that comes to mind. Be sure to include that the Creator of the universe thinks you're His special princess. —HB

Day 34

I Am Peaceful (Part 1)

Peace I leave with you;
My peace I give to you;
not as the world gives do I give to you.
Do not let your heart be troubled,
nor let it be fearful.

John 14:27 (NASB)

A true gift is something we receive which we did not work or pay for. A true gift is also something that cannot be taken back by the giver. There is no contract involved in a true gift. It is a one-way transaction that cannot be revoked.

A few years ago, I threw my husband a big surprise party for his 40th birthday. He had no clue it was coming, and we all hid throughout the living room so we could jump out and surprise him with our thoughtfulness. Now, it was our intention to be a blessing to him, but he could have chosen not to cooperate. He could have seen all of the guests once he walked in the door, and run right back out. He could have decided to worry about all the efforts we made for him and felt too guilty to enjoy our gift of love. He could have gotten angry and sulked during all of the festivities, and the yummy catered food, and missed the frivolity that was designed to be a blessing to him. Luckily, he did choose to enjoy and receive the love and gifts that were lavished on him, and it made his heart glad to know he was so appreciated.

God's gifts for us operate the same way. We can choose to receive His gifts of love, mercy, grace, and forgiveness, or we can believe that we have to earn them, or even that we can lose them if we mess up. God sent Jesus to be perfection for us so that we don't have to be perfect to enjoy God's blessings in our lives. Take some time right now to ask God what you have been trying to earn what He is trying to give to you freely. Now, receive it in full, knowing that His Son makes you worthy to receive it and it is His good pleasure to give His blessings to you! —SF

I Am Not Troubled or Fearful (Part 2)

Peace I leave with you;
My peace I give to you;
not as the world gives do I give to you.
Do not let your heart be troubled,
nor let it be fearful.

John 14:27 (NASB)

A few years ago, my eldest son asked me a really good question about peace. My husband and I have always taught our children that the peace Jesus left for us is a gift. But we also taught them that they have to stay away from worry and fear. My son put these two things together and asked me why we have to make sure not to worry if Jesus' peace is a gift that we don't earn? I was unsure how to answer him until I heard the Holy Spirit speak to my heart this scripture in John 14. He reminded me that there are two parts to all of the blessings of God. He does His part, and we have to do our part for the fullness of the blessings to manifest in our lives. An example of this is our salvation through Jesus Christ. Jesus died for our sins over 2000 years ago, but that salvation doesn't manifest to us personally until we do our part and accept it as the truth for us.

The same principle works with the peace of God in our lives. His part is to do everything necessary for us to qualify to receive it freely from God through Christ. Our part is to receive it and keep our heart from being troubled or fearful. When we give in to worry and fear, we are actually letting go of the peace we have in Christ, and leaning on our own efforts to solve our problems or the challenges we see before us. This is a self-discipline issue. but we can grow in our habit of relying on God and trusting in His goodness and peace as we practice. Choose today to lean on the peace Jesus gave you, and refuse to be troubled or fearful in your heart! God loves you! —SF

Day 36

I Have Hope

For I know the plans I have for you, declares the Lord,
plans for welfare, and not for evil,
to give you a future and a hope.

Jeremiah 29:11 (ESV)

Too often hope recedes quickly in time of trials. Many who search for hope in this world through connections, friends, money, or material possessions quickly fall when one or all of the aforementioned things dwindle. But it doesn't have to be this way.

The Lord provides endless hope—a hope that doesn't change because we messed up, or things are messing up around us. This hope doesn't go away because you lose your job, lose your family, or your house burns down.

Our hope is in Jesus! "For the believer there is hope beyond the grave, because Jesus Christ has opened the door to heaven for us by His death and resurrection." -Billy Graham[2]

Every day is a new day and when there is hope in Jesus, we can see a future. We can see that trials and tribulations are only momentary and will end. Hope in Jesus is what keeps us moving and motivated to get out of bed when we may feel hopeless.

Right now, hope is yours to grasp. Jesus's hand is reaching out to you and this time, take it!! Lean in to His embrace and revive your hope in Him. Pray to receive the ever-lasting hope He has for you! And this time, fully receive what the Lord has for you! —DM

I Don't Worry

*Therefore humble yourselves
under the mighty hand of God,
that He may exalt you at the proper time,
casting all your anxiety on Him,
because He cares for you.*

1 Peter 5:6-7 (NASB)

God's timing is perfect. Let me repeat that for emphasis: God's. Timing. Is. Perfect.

It is always a temptation in our lives to look at our circumstances and wonder if God is still paying attention to us. When things don't go our way, or the help we believe we need doesn't materialize, we can be taken aback, believing that either we missed it, or God missed it. But never forget:

God's. Timing. Is. Perfect.

We don't know everything. We don't see everything that is going on. We can't control anyone else involved. The part we do see is only a small portion of the whole plan. So we might as well accept that we are going to have to trust in God, in His good and perfect timing, goodness, and love for us in order for us to enjoy this wonderful life He has given to us. We can fuss. We can fume. We can fret. We can try harder to be and do what He has planned for us, but in the end we have to trust that….God's. Timing. Is. Perfect.

Peter gives us the perfect reason to trust in His goodness toward us His perfect timing: He cares for us. The God of the universe, Who flung the stars and planets farther than we can even see yet, and knows how many hairs we have on our heads, cares for us. Meditate today on the truth of God's love for you and that His timing really is perfect for you. You can trust Him. He won't let you down. —SF

I Am Renewed

And you shall know the truth,
and the truth shall make you free.

John 8:32 (NKJV)

How do you see yourself? Do you look in the mirror and see all your imperfections like you're broken–unfit for His use? Or, do you see the beautiful woman you are, His masterpiece, loved and cherished by your Heavenly Father?

Many believe the lie that "I'm broken." The truth is, you're God's Masterpiece created in Christ for good works. Friends, we've believed a lie that's created a false image of ourselves for far too long–it's time to change that false belief. Our Heavenly Father created each of us as unique individuals. We're an exclusive original. But, if we don't believe that, we'll never walk in the fullness of who God designed us to be.

When you believe something long enough, it gets hardwired into your brain. But the good news is, God made it possible for you to rewire your mind so you can believe the truth. Then that truth will set you free (John 8:32)!

How do you rewire your thoughts? Renew your mind (Romans 12:2). Renew means renovation: complete change for the better. It's like home renovation shows that take an old and decrepit house and change it into something astonishing. That's what you're doing when you renew your mind to God's truth. You can't hold a negative thought and a positive thought at the same time. Each time the lie comes to mind, replace it with the truth of what God says about you. That's renewing and renovating it!

Change doesn't happen overnight, but change comes with consistency. And, now that you know the truth, you're set free from the lies that have held you back. You're ready for the good things that He's designed for you to walk in!

Pick one lie that you've believed. Now, find scriptures that show you the truth about yourself. Write out each scripture, read it over and over, and commit it to heart. That will begin the renovation process. —HB

Day 39

I Am A Slave to Righteousness

Being then made free from sin,
ye became the servants of righteousness.

Romans 6:18 (KJV)

Slavery in previous centuries was a horrible practice whereby one people enslaved another people to do their will. Slaves weren't entitled to free choice of activity, but had to obey the desires of their masters. We all know what it feels like to be a slave to sin— that sick feeling in the pit of your stomach; that belief we just can't escape the darkness in our own hearts; that hopelessness that no matter how hard we try, we will never be free of the sin we try desperately to hide.

We can understand what that type of slavery feels like because we all lived it before Christ came into our lives and we may feel it even now. Paul is telling us here in Romans 6 that something transpired which changed all of that for us forever: our citizenship changed. Our state of unrighteous sinfulness was removed and replaced! Now that we are in Christ, we are slaves to THAT reality of righteousness. And just as surely as our slavery to sin was without release or escape, our present citizenship as a joint-heir with Christ and a servant of righteousness is iron-clad. That's right, no matter what trips us up, we will inevitably fall into His arms of grace and love and acceptance. We have been bought with a very high price, so now we cannot be stolen away again into bondage to sin. We are permanently chained by His grace to right-standing in His eyes.

Let your heart rejoice in that knowledge! Know that no matter how hard you try, you cannot earn His favor, but just as surely, you cannot lose it once it is given. Hallelujah! —SF

I Am Content

"Not that I speak from want,
for I have learned to be content
in whatever circumstances I am.
I know how to get along with humble means,
and I also know how to live in prosperity;
in any and every circumstance
I have learned the secret of being filled and going hungry,
both of having abundance and suffering need.
I can do all things through Him who strengthens me."

Philippians 4:11-13 (NASB)

Until Jesus returns at the end of this age, there will always be situations and circumstances that make us uncomfortable or unhappy. There will always be ways in which our life could be improved. There will always be people that seem to really get under our skin. But Jesus died for us to have life and have it in abundance (John 10:10), so there must be some way we can live content and fulfilled lives in the midst of these issues.

A working definition of "content" is "satisfied, happy, and gratified" and it is within our power to control the level of contentment we enjoy.

Our contentment in life is a direct result of where our internal focus is. If we are meditating on (thinking about, reasoning about) what we believe is wrong in our lives, what we need to change, or what we are missing, we will feel dissatisfied, unhappy, and restless. If we turn our eyes to Jesus, we will find Him to be all we need to make us truly contented. It's a skill we get to practice every day.

Let's start by making a list of 5 things you are truly thankful for right now, and repeat this throughout your day as needed! —SF

Day 41

———

I Am A Witness

The woman then left her waterpot,
went her way into the city,
and said to the men,
"Come, see a Man who told me
all things that I ever did.
Could this be the Christ?"
Then they went out of the city and came to Him.

John 4:28-30 (NKJV)

The woman of Samaria, like all of us, was just going about her own business taking care of her own needs her own way. She was using her relationships with men to fill the void in her heart and was rejected by the religious people of her day because her sin of adultery and fornication was "worse" than theirs. She was forced to come to the well in the heat of the day, away from the condemning townspeople, and found herself fully laid bare before the Son of God.

Jesus met her there, in the center of her world, just as she was: lonely, unfulfilled, and searching. He offered her living water that never runs out—Himself. She took Him up on His offer. He didn't even ask her to give up what she had been clinging to only moments before: her own ability to provide for herself— her own waterpot. But because she saw Him, listened to Him, and received Him, she decided to leave all she had without a moment's hesitation. She was totally transformed in that single moment of grace.

This transformation was so complete that she became the shining witness Jesus used to draw this entire town to Himself. This once discarded, unloved, sinful woman was now a princess of peace as she surrendered her broken, empty heart to be filled with His love and grace. She didn't need the old ways of living anymore and didn't give it a second thought.

Let the fullness of God's goodness toward you in Christ transform you in the same way today! —SF

Day 42

I Am Grateful

Rejoice always, pray without ceasing,
in everything give thanks;
for this is the will of God in Christ Jesus for you.

1 Thessalonians 5:16-18 (NKJV)

Emotions are not bad in themselves. Our Creator gave us emotions. They allow you to feel what you're thinking. If you're thinking worrying thoughts, it produces anxious emotions. On the other spectrum, peaceful thoughts create peaceful emotions. Joyful thoughts produce joyful emotions. You can proactively choose thoughts to produce more of the emotions you want to experience.

Gratitude is one of the best ways to proactively banish worrisome thoughts and produce joyful, peaceful thoughts. God tells us in everything give thanks. He's not saying be thankful FOR the circumstance, just be thankful IN it. Why? Gratitude reminds you of all that is going right in your life and all He's done for you.

During WWII, Jimmy Durante did a benefit show for the US troops. He told the coordinators he only had a few minutes to stay and then had to leave for his next commitment. His few minutes were up, but he kept going. 15 minutes went by and then 30. The applause grew louder. He took his last bow and walked off stage. When asked why he stayed, Jimmy answered, "I can show you the reason that I stayed. Look on the front row." Two men were clapping loudly and cheerfully. Each man had lost an arm in the war. One man lost his left arm and the other man lost his right arm. Together, they were clapping–having the time of their lives.

We have so much we can be grateful for. Here are two simple ways you can proactively choose gratitude:

1. Start a Gratitude Journal (on paper or digitally). Each morning, write 5 things you're thankful for. As you experience blessings throughout the day, write it down. Now you can go back and remind yourself what you're thankful for.
2. Write thank-you notes. Let people know the gift they are in your life. You can even write a thank you note to God. —HB

Day 43

———

I Am Strongly Equipped

For though we walk in the flesh,
we do not war according to the flesh,
for the weapons of our warfare are not of the flesh,
but divinely powerful for the destruction of fortresses.

2 Corinthians 10:3-4 (NASB)

Mother, you are not at the mercy of our culture or even your own parenting abilities when it comes to parenting your children. God has provided you with mighty weapons in Christ that are way more powerful than the world's way of doing things. Instead of worrying, doubting, "pop culture parenting," or sticking your head in the sand and hoping for the best, use God's weapons and ensure victory!

So how do we do that? Find God's promises about your children in His Word. He wants to fulfill them for you! Some examples include:

> *All your children shall be taught by the Lord,*
> *And great shall be the peace of your children. Isaiah 54:13 (ESV)*

> *Train up a child in the way he should go, And when he is old he will not depart from it. Proverbs 22:6(ESV)*

> *Even the captives of the mighty man will be taken away,*
> *And the prey of the tyrant will be rescued;*
> *For I will contend with the one who contends with you,*
> *And I will save your sons. Isaiah 49:25(ESV)*

Speak these promises out loud and often when you are tempted to worry. Speak them to your children. Speak them, and only them, about your children.

We aren't smart enough to defeat the enemy of our souls with our own reasoning. We just don't have it. But God has given us the most powerful force in all of Creation if we will just use it—HIS WORD! Quit believing the devil's report about your kids and start believe what God says and you will see it! —SF

I Look to Jesus

*Therefore, since we have so great a
cloud of witnesses surrounding us,
let us also lay aside every encumbrance
and the sin which so easily entangles us,
and let us run with endurance the race
that is set before us, fixing our eyes on Jesus,
the author and perfecter of faith,
who for the joy set before Him endured the cross,
despising the shame, and has sat down
at the right hand of the throne of God.*

Hebrews 12:1-2 (NASB)

My family had a wonderful trip to the beach Christmas 2018 during a really challenging season in our personal lives. As my husband and I were taking a walk down the beach and reflecting on all the issues we had before us, we came upon a section of the beach where a freshwater river met the salty ocean. The waves produced a nasty, stinky brown foam and it wasn't particularly picturesque or pleasant to say the least! As I looked at the ugliness created from the vigorous mixture of fresh and salt water, I mentally noted how that's what our life had been lately. Troubles kept coming at us—not unlike wave after wave when you walk a little too far out into the surf and can't quite get your balance. The Lord spoke to my heart and said, "Look to the horizon." I looked up and saw the clear ocean ahead—stable, smooth, unchanging, unwavering. I looked back down at the tumultuous brown foam that still filled most of my view and I didn't really see the connection. It wasn't until a few weeks later upon further reflection with a friend that I realized the truth God was sharing with me. When my focus is filled with Jesus and His faith, righteousness, power, and plan, I won't even hardly notice the dirty foam at my feet.

Another thing God reminded me later is that there was so much food available for the wildlife at that juncture between fresh and salty water. Life was everywhere! Birds were eating the small creatures that thrived in that brackish environment, and the water was teeming with fruitfulness!

Let's focus on Jesus when life is hard, knowing that the challenging areas in our lives can lead to the most growth and fruitfulness. As we fix our eyes on Jesus, we won't even notice the waves! —SF

Day 45

I Am Blessed

For the Lord God is a sun and shield;
The Lord gives grace and glory;
No good thing does He withhold from
those who walk uprightly.

Psalm 84:11 (NASB)

The capacity to receive the love of God by the human heart is inexhaustible. We were literally designed by God to receive His love for us. We crave it, even more than food or water, and we can't function without it. When we walk through life without His ever-present favor on us and pleasure in us, we seek that love and acceptance through what we accomplish, what we eat, who we love, who or what we know, how we act, who we please, and what we look like.

But God's heart, His desire for us, is to walk every minute of our lives fully aware of His deep and abiding love toward us, and His superabounding favor on us released in our lives through what Jesus did on the cross. How do we do that? We turn the attention of our hearts to Jesus and what He has already done for us, and we receive it for ourselves.

If I make my children a yummy loaf of homemade bread, fresh out of the oven, but they won't take any of it, it does them no good and I am sad because they wouldn't enjoy what I spent time and energy creating for them out of the love of my heart. In the same way, we have to accept that what Jesus did, what God did, was for us. Let it become part of you, part of your thinking, part of your believing. It will change you forever. Meditate on these scriptures today:

> For as many as are the promises of God, in Him they are yes; therefore also through Him is our Amen to the glory of God through us. 2 Corinthians 1:20(NASB)

> What then shall we say to these things? If God is for us, who is against us? Romans 8:31(NASB) —SF

Day 46

ℐ Am Blessed

*Blessed be the God and Father of our Lord Jesus Christ,
who has blessed us with every spiritual blessing in the
heavenly places in Christ, just as He chose us in Him
before the foundation of the world, that we should be
holy and without blame before Him, in love having
predestined us to adoption as sons by Jesus Christ to
Himself, according to the good pleasure of His will,
to the praise of the glory of His grace,
by which He made us accepted in the Beloved.*

Ephesians 1:3-6 (NASB)

When Adam and Eve sinned in the Garden of Eden, they interrupted God's plans of blessing them and their children. When Jesus purchased us back on the Cross, He brought us back into the blessings of God in such a way that it is no longer dependent on us to maintain that position or relationship. Jesus' righteousness was the final word on who we now are to God. He took our sinful and rebellious relationship with God and gave us His relationship with the Father, so that now no matter what we do, we are always accepted and beloved. This was His gift to us! God loves us so much! His plans for us are too great for us to comprehend in this lifetime. Even though the mercies and grace He pours out on our lives will take an eternity for us to fully receive, He wants us to start today!

During a very hard financial season for my husband and I in our early marriage, I was struggling to find money with which to buy groceries for our family. We had two young children at home at the time and payday was over a week away. I prayed and begged God for help and listened. I poured out my needs and stretched my little faith out to grasp the blessings of provision God promised to us in His Word. For a few days, I kept getting an image in my spirit of a green CD holder we had. I just couldn't shake it. It was really weird, to be honest! Finally, I went and found it in my husband's nightstand and opened it. There was $100 in it! My husband had put the money in it a few months prior at a family Christmas gathering and had forgotten all about it. God's provision was there all along, but I had to ask, I had to listen, I had to believe, and I had to respond in faith.

That testimony speaks to us about all the blessings we have in Christ that are ours, but we haven't discovered yet. We may even have known some of these promises in the past, but have forgotten all that was included in our inheritance. Spend time now asking Him to meet your needs because of who you are now in Christ! —SF

Day 47

I Am Not Alone

Be of sober spirit, be on the alert.
Your adversary, the devil, prowls around
like a roaring lion, seeking someone to devour.
But resist him, firm in your faith,
knowing that the same experiences of suffering
are being accomplished by your brethren
who are in the world.

1 Peter 5:8-9 (NASB)

You are not alone in your striving against the attacks of the enemy. The devil would have you believe that you are the only one and no one else understands what you are going through, but that is simply not true! We all struggle from time to time. We all suffer under injustice and attacks from time to time. As we develop friendships and fellowship with other believers, we will come across others who have been through similar experiences and come out the other side in victory! Hearing their stories will strengthen our faith, and encourage us to continue walking in confident assurance that God is with us and everything will be alright.

I remember going to Bible studies with other women as a younger woman, and marveling at the wisdom and experience of the older ladies of the group. When I would share a challenge or situation I was dealing with, there would invariably be one or two other women who had been through a similar issue in their lives. They would share God's Word and a wonderful testimony about God's faithfulness to them in their situation. I would always leave encouraged and confident that the same God Who brought them through would bring me through too.

Take some time this week and share some of the struggles or secret sins you are encountering with a trusted mature woman of God or Bible study group. If you don't have a friend or group that you believe will keep your matters private, pray and ask God to bring you to a mature woman of God or Bible study group that will be a source of help and hope for you. God will answer you and is always ready to bless you when you choose to follow His path! —SF

Day 48

I Am Secure

Do not fear, for I am with you;
Do not anxiously look about you,
for I am your God. I will strengthen you,
surely I will help you,
Surely I will uphold you
with My righteous right hand.

Isaiah 41:10 (NASB)

We all have the choice to put our trust in whatever we want to. We can trust in our friends, our intelligence, our abilities, our experience, our money, our family, our success, and our looks. Or, we can choose to put our trust in the only One incapable of lying, and Who is so incredibly full of love for us, it would be impossible for Him to do anything but help and bless us.

All of the promises we read about in the Old Testament give us glimpses of God's character and His love toward humanity. The specifics of each promise might be directed toward Israel for a single purpose at the time, but the care, faithfulness, and purposes of God revealed in them apply to us as well!

It's your choice, but your choice determines your results. If you keep relying on yourself, you will get limited results. If you will choose to trust in Jesus and His love for you, you will be overwhelmed with His love and faithfulness. I know it's scary, but choose Jesus anyway. The most powerful and best decisions are rarely the easy and safe ones.

Choose an area in your life today to completely surrender to God. As He shows Himself faithful to you, write it down so you won't forget! —SF

Day 49

I Am Blessed Beyond Measure

So I answered them and said to them,
"The God of heaven will give us success;
therefore we His servants will arise and build,
but you have no portion,
right or memorial in Jerusalem."

Nehemiah 2:20 (NASB)

A cup-bearer for the king was going to rebuild a wall of protection around the Lord's people. One man. One idea. But, he had one true God.

Who are the "them" in today's verse? They were mockers, ridiculers, and naysayers, and they worked to delay Nehemiah in his mission. Nehemiah could have allowed "them" to break down his servant-heart and taken their degrading words to heart, but he didn't. No, not this guy. I imagine him firmly planting his feet in the sandy ground, looking them straight in the eye, and saying, "The God of heaven Himself will give us success...."

Have you ever truly wondered about how a bricklayer builds a wall? Maybe you haven't been particularly curious, but when I read this verse in Nehemiah, I pondered on how repetitive and boring laying bricks has got to be! Over and over, the same mundane task, pulling at the muscles and exhausting the brain. Sounds like a high school sandwich-making job I had once. Same sandwich, same process, different day.

But there was this co-worker who brought joy everywhere she went, and boy, did she love what she was doing no matter what the task! As I complained, she blessed me with her words of encouragement. Once, she looked at a sandwich I had made, and before she wrapped it up, she loudly called attention to everyone saying, "This young lady just made the best sandwich I've ever seen. Let's applaud her!" She took the dull and made it a delight. I felt like a huge success in that moment.

We will rise and build. The God of heaven will give you success in the simple everyday tasks and even in the complex, momentous tasks. Give these tasks to the Lord! And He will bless them beyond measure. — DM

I Am Seeking God First

But seek first His kingdom and His righteousness, and all these things will be added to you.

Matthew 6:33 (NASB)

God is so good! He wants you to have every blessing He originally created for Adam and Eve and their children! He wants you to have more than enough money, food, clothing, time, strength, peace, joy, and everything else that makes life very good! Because you have made Jesus your Lord, you have received a new heart that seeks after God and His kingdom naturally. Now, because you have a new spiritual connection with your Father God, you deeply want to please Him in all respects. Having this attitude places you squarely in God's Blessing Zone! He wants to pour out His goodness and grace on you in every area of your life, but you have to keep Him first in all things, because these things Jesus was talking about above can easily become idols.

If wealth, food, clothing, popularity, or any of these other things become first in your life, it will destroy you and God's good plans for your life. In this verse, Jesus is showing the Jews that our Father God truly does love us and wants the best for us, but if we are drawn away from seeking Him first in our lives, we are actually preventing Him from adding these things to us. There are times when our foolishness asks God for things we don't fully understand, like a specific person for a spouse, or a special job we think would be better for us. God knows the future and the current state of our hearts and those around us, and God would never give us what would hurt us, even if we beg Him for it! The good news is that the new spirit of an adopted child that He put in our hearts longs to follow Him first, and doesn't want to worship anyone or anything but Him! Humanity absolutely can't do any of this in the flesh—in our own human efforts. Years of religious duty upheld by the Jewish leaders and years of depraved immorality by the Gentile nations showed us how fruitless that was before Jesus came to bring new life in His blood. As we receive all that He is for us, our hearts are finally set free to be the child of God that can receive His goodness without turning away from His glory! Say, "I am seeking God first" today when you are tempted to look for peace elsewhere."—SF

Day 51

I Am Established

In righteousness you will be established;
You will be far from oppression, for you will not fear;
And from terror, for it will not come near you.

Isaiah 54:14 (NASB)

I grew up in the country of South Korea, in the city of Seoul. My father was in the US Army, and we were stationed there in the 80s. My mom and I used to go shopping downtown at least once a week. It was always such a fun time to witness all of the street vendors showcasing their fabrics or their culinary delights. The amazing Korean culture was on full display as we saw, heard, and smelled so many new foods and products. It was all so wonderful to enjoy and experience and I am eternally grateful for it. The only annoyance we ever encountered was when we were on a mission and were pressed for time. The shop owners would try and draw us in to their booths and would entice us with a "special deal," but we were undeterred as we hunted for that specific item.

There are a lot of sellers in the marketplace of life. These days, many seem to be peddling fear, anxiety, and uncertainty. The news would have us believe that the world will end in a decade if we don't do what they tell us to right now. We are led to believe that our political system is in shambles and hopelessly broken without the help of certain politicians. It is in the devil's best interest to keep us fearful, worried, and hurried.

The goods news is you don't have to buy any of it. You can walk right by that booth trying to sell you things you don't want without feeling like you are missing out, uninformed, or foolish. Real foolishness is in believing what the world says over what God says. Take a moment to review whatever may be worrying you and stealing your peace and find out what God says about the matter. He is right! —SF

I Am His Princess

*…having predestined us to adoption as sons
by Jesus Christ to Himself,
according to the good pleasure of His will,
to the praise of the glory of His grace,
by which He made us accepted in the Beloved.*

Ephesians 1:5-6 (NKJV)

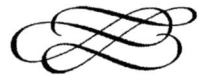

Have you ever had one of your friends, or maybe even your child, get down on themselves in front of you? You heard them rake themselves over the coals for making a mistake; maybe they lamented about how ugly or unwanted they are. How did that make you feel? Did your heart hurt for them? Did you try and convince them to see the truth because you knew those were lies they were believing?

How about you? Have you ever gotten down on yourself for the same thing? You made a mistake and you treated yourself as if the world was going to end (I've done that one!). You were trying on clothes in the morning and were so angry at yourself because nothing fit (I've done that one too!). Have you ever thought how our Heavenly Father feels when we, His children, treat ourselves like that? He feels like you did when you saw your friend or child treat themselves poorly. His heart aches and longs for us to believe the truth that we are His chosen, special person–cherished by Him.

My friend, you are His daughter. You are accepted in the Beloved. Beloved refers to what God prefers. Your Heavenly Father prefers you! His greatest desire was to have you as a daughter. You're a daughter of the King. That makes you a princess! Think of yourself as His princess. Treat yourself like His princess. Speak to yourself like you're His princess. Because that is what you are–beloved royalty.

Remember, when you make a mistake or want to say something negative about yourself–stop. Remind yourself of His grace. Remind yourself you're His beloved princess. Then, speak to yourself like you are. —HB

Day 53

I Am the Salt of the Earth

You are the salt of the earth;
but if the salt has become tasteless,
how can it be made salty again?
It is no longer good for anything,
except to be thrown out and
trampled under foot by men.

Matthew 5:13 (NASB)

Salt has been used for centuries as a preservative and a flavor enhancer when added to perishable food like meat, fruits, or vegetables. Adding salt to some foods can even enhance the sweetness of them. If you have ever enjoyed salt on a slice of watermelon, you have already experienced this effect firsthand!

There is much on this sinful, broken earth that would lead people to hopelessness and despair if we Christians were not here to share God's love. Our sweet countenance at the check-out line, our friendly smile in the waiting room, or our joyful presence in the school pick-up line can add a sweetness to the lives of those around us that we too often discount. We aren't sent here to make the world palatable to God—Jesus did that—but to make life on earth tolerable to those who don't yet know Him. Their lives would be bitter and hopeless without our salty influence of faith, hope and love. We are powerful as we reflect His love, peace, and joy to the world around us, and our salty influence shines a light on the goodness and love of our Father.

We add a preserving influence as we seek God's ways of blessing instead of the world's culture of death and destruction. Sin always destroys, and the sins which are embraced and encouraged in our culture are sent to destroy those loved and sought by God. Allow the love, joy, and peace of God to flow through you today as you go about your business. Watch how spreading the love of God to others, by His grace, changes their countenance and brings them joy!—SF

Day 54

I Am Chosen of God

So, as those who have been chosen of God,
holy and beloved, put on a heart of compassion,
kindness, humility, gentleness and patience;
bearing with one another, and forgiving each other,
whoever has a complaint against anyone;
just as the Lord forgave you,
so also should you.

Colossians 3:12-13 (NASB)

Anyone who has ever played a game of kickball or baseball with other kids during recess or PE knows the sting of being the last one picked for a team. Or if you were ever passed over for the big Homecoming Dance or Prom, you know that sting of rejection as well. We all want to feel loved and accepted by our peers, even wanted for our looks or our abilities. Thankfully, God doesn't see as man sees—He sees our hearts and our potential. And He saw you before you were even born, and He said, "I want THAT ONE!" Before you could do anything to earn His love for you, He loved you more than anything. Knowing and believing in this level of love is honestly overwhelming! It defies our understanding and overcomes our reasoning abilities—but it is the absolute truth. God goes on to say here in Colossians that not only are we chosen of God, He has made us holy and beloved as well! It just keeps getting better!

Once we have received these truths, we find it infinitely easier to put on a heart of compassion, kindness, humility, gentleness, and patience. Bearing with others is no problem when we receive all the love and forbearance we have in Christ. Forgiving others is a cinch when we remember how much we have been forgiven! The key to walking in all of these Godly characteristics is found at the beginning of this reading—knowing we are chosen of God, holy and beloved.

Speak that over yourself today and believe it. —SF

Day 55

I Am Wise

If any of you lacks wisdom,
you should ask God, who gives generously
to all without finding fault,
and it will be given to you.

James 1:5 (NIV)

Often I find myself needing wisdom but searching the wrong sources for the answer. I lean on a family member, a friend, the internet, or someone with earthly experience about the situation with which I need guidance. Why is it that I am so easily able to pick up the phone or open the computer, but choose to pray or search God's Holy Word second or last? (Gasp!)

I used to believe that I wasn't worthy of the gifts the Lord has. But He says He will give "generously to all without finding fault." The wisdom the Lord has for us will overpower any wisdom we might glean from cultural or worldly influences. The knowledge and the understanding of the Lord is more powerful than anything on this earth.

I meet with a Christ-filled mentor monthly and sometimes even weekly. There was a time when I was praying and crying out to the Lord for direction, and I phoned her daily. She always, and I mean always, says these words, "Have you prayed about it first?" She used wisdom by pointing me to Jesus first and then suggested gleaning wisdom from Godly people. Not the other way around. Each time I have met with my mentor, God meets me with His wisdom and knowledge. And it is always exactly what I need to hear.

Today, I want you to see yourself as the wise, gifted woman you are! The Lord has equipped you with knowledge and understanding through His Word. Is there something about which you are lacking in wisdom? Right now, ask God to reveal to you the scriptures you need. Ask Him to bring to you the wisdom of Godly people in your life from whom you may seek guidance. The Lord wants to give you wisdom!! All you have to do is ask for it! —DM

I Am Loved

*And we have known and believed
the love that God has for us.
God is love, and he who abides in love
abides in God, and God in him.*

1 John 4:16 (NKJV)

We may know something, but not actually believe it. There is a difference in knowing that planes fly and getting on a plane and expecting it to carry you through the air to where you want to go. If you choose to ride the train on a long trip instead of actually buying a plane ticket and boarding the plane, your belief in that plane's safety is just a theory. Unless we are convinced of a truth to the point that it changes our behavior, we don't actually believe it.

James mentions this when he says that "faith without accompanying works is dead" in James 2. If our belief system isn't engaging our actions, it isn't real faith. This fact isn't meant to condemn us, but to help us determine if we truly believe in God's Word or not. If we find it impossible to act on what we have read in His Word, we need to acknowledge the fact that we don't really believe it yet. Once we have faced that fact, we can repent for our unbelief and choose to open our hearts to the truths found in His Word. As we meditate on God's Word, believing it to be the truth, we will find our faith and belief system agreeing with God, and our actions will change to accompany those new beliefs. It is an amazing work that the Word of God can accomplish in our hearts as we know and believe the truth!

Let's act like God really does love us today, because He really does! Put your weight on it. Expect God to do things for you that He would only do if He really does love you—such as working in your life to meet your needs, giving you the wisdom to parent effectively, and showing you how to work out that problem you've been wrestling with. If He really does love you, and He does, it will actually manifest in your life when you know it and believe it. —SF

Day 57

I Am Healed

But He was wounded for our transgressions,
He was bruised for our iniquities;
The chastisement for our peace was upon Him,
And by His stripes we are healed.

Isaiah 53:5 (NKJV)

When we consider all the parts of the crucifixion, there were more things going on than just the shedding of blood for the remission of our sins. If we look as Isaiah's prophecy regarding the death of the Messiah, he lists out the Messiah's work in more areas than just for our transgressions. Saint Peter brings this same Scripture up in 1 Peter 2:24 and alludes to part of Christ's work being the purchase of our health and healing. In fact, the only thing required for our eternal salvation from Hell was the payment of Jesus' sinless blood—His death. But Jesus didn't just die the horrible death of crucifixion for our eternal salvation, He also purposefully took 39 strikes on His back with a "cat of nine tails" for our physical health. That was not accidental. He wants us healed. He paid extra for us to have it.

His bloody wounds paid for our sins. His bruising—which is actually bleeding internally—paid for our internal, emotional weaknesses and wounds. His open shame and punishment provided us with His peace and acceptance by God. The stripes on His back paid for our physical health. He didn't just give up His life-blood for you, but suffered in His body and soul as well.

His redemption of us was four-fold and complete, and at His second coming, our final enemy—death—will be completely eradicated as well!

Thank Jesus today for your health! —SF

Day 58

I Have Peace with My Enemies

When a man's ways please the Lord,
He makes even his enemies to be at peace with him.

Proverbs 16:7 (NKJV)

When I was in my 20's, I worked for a prominent testing company who gave important tests to those seeking to advance in their careers—most critically, in the medical and business fields. The stress level and tension could be cut with a knife as people were very, very nervous. We were a team of four women, working two at a time, and we knew our job was to make everyone feel comfortable and make sure the tests and testing room were secure. We were responsible if anything happened!

On my first day, my manager introduced me to the system. She was stern, but very kind and funny. After a couple of weeks, my manager's attitude began to become unbearable. She micromanaged, belittled, and ridiculed us in everything we did. Working at the testing company was excruciating, and we were confined to such a small office, there was nowhere to hide.

One particular day, I left the office and cried hysterically in my car. I prayed to the Lord about my manager. I prayed that He would cover her in love and save her from whatever it was that was hurting her because hurting people hurt people. At the end of that prayer, I decided to give them my two weeks notice. That same evening, I received a call from a coworker that our manager was in the hospital.

For the next three weeks, my manager called me directly and shared with me what was happening in her life to cause her anger and behavior. She and I prayed together over her situation. She apologized to each one of us. I wonder, if I had not prayed over my manager, would I have picked up the phone when she called? See, there is something about praying over your enemies. The Lord filled me with compassion and understanding that He was doing something in her.

When it was time for me to leave that job, she and I stayed connected for many years. What enemy could you pray over today? — DM

Day 59

I Am An Encourager

*Let no unwholesome word proceed from your mouth,
but only such a word as is good for edification
according to the need of the moment,
so that it will give grace to those who hear.*

Ephesians 4:29 (NASB)

Our words are very powerful. We were made in the image of the God who literally spoke everything in our universe into existence. Our words can lift the discouraged, or shackle the downtrodden. We have the freedom in Christ to choose which source we are going to draw from—our flesh which only produces death and corruption, or the Spirit, which brings life and peace (Romans 8:6).

Mark Twain is often quoted as saying, "I can live for two months on a good compliment!" I think he had learned the value of spoken words of encouragement. It is possible that he learned this through experiencing the positive effects of a sincere word of encouragement or from the negative affects of a discouraging word. Either way, this world-famous author learned the power of words and thrived when good words were spoken over him.

Let's not use our words to bind leashes on people, but wings. Let our words be a source of encouragement, words that would cast a greater vision in the lives of those around us. Let not our words hold people back; instead let's say, "You can do this!" Let's avoid, "You can't do that!" or "You were never good at this." We don't know what God's plans for them are. Our words can be used to encourage and be uplifting, not drag others down. Let's have God's vision not man's vision. With God, all things are possible. Don't prove people wrong, prove God right. —SF

I Am A Fellowshipper

What we have seen and heard we proclaim to you also,
so that you too may have fellowship with us;
and indeed our fellowship is with the Father,
and with His Son Jesus Christ.

1 John 1:3 (NASB)

Going to church isn't the same thing as knowing God personally. It's just a place where other believers have set the stage for you to encounter Him yourself. It's like going to the grocery store to pick up some food to eat. Every area has been organized, cleaned, and set for. You could walk down every aisle full to the top with every food imaginable and still walk out without anything in your shopping bag when you're done. While at church, you need to open your heart to the possibilities that God loves you, God wants to connect with you, and Jesus is real. Then He has your permission to start loading up with His goodness. Give Him a chance! He really does love you.

God values your relationships with other believers as well. He wants you to know aspects of His character that can only be expressed to you by other people in the body of Christ. He never intended for a Christian to live life alone, but in a wonderful family called the church. Our attitude toward the church experience greatly influences how and what we can receive from it. Fellowship with other believers is so vital to the healthy life of a Christian, God made it mandatory (see Hebrews 10:25)!

Make the decision this week to start regularly attending a Bible-teaching church near you, if you aren't already. If you are, look for new ways to connect with other believers. You won't regret it! —SF

Day 61

———

I Am Forgetful

Brethren, I do not regard myself
as having laid hold of it yet;
but one thing I do:
forgetting what lies behind and reaching forward
to what lies ahead, I press on toward the goal
for the prize of the upward call of God in Christ Jesus.

Philippians 3:13-14 (NASB)

Every day we have a choice to make. We can choose to press on in our faith walk with God, or we can meditate on and wallow in our past. This is a real temptation for us because we want to do something now that can possibly change our past poor decisions. We want to heal the wounds we caused others or others caused us.

Paul had been directly or indirectly responsible for the deaths of Christians as a leader of the Pharisees, as they persecuted the early church for years in and around Jerusalem. He had much in his past that he was rightfully ashamed of when he finally understood that he was wrong. It could have derailed his ministry if he hadn't learned this important skill: forget what lies behind. God had mercifully forgiven Paul for his murderous behavior toward His children. Paul had to make the purposeful choice to do the same and let it all go.

Paul could count Jesus' payment on the cross as the payment for his sins and forget the past, or he could spend the rest of his life trying to make up for the sins he committed and live in self-condemnation, fear, and regret every single day. We have this same choice to make every day as well. As much as we would love to, we aren't able to change our history, and, if we hold onto it, our past can drag us down and keep us from the fullness of God's plans for us. Paul decided to let go of all of his past regrets to God, and fully receive what Jesus offers to us as well: complete forgiveness. As we press in to what God offers to us through Christ, His healing can flow to our hearts. His healing and restoration can flow to us, and those we may have hurt along the way. Paul tells us from his experience that the first step is to forget the past and press on toward Jesus. God can help you do that.

Confess it all to Him right now and ask for His help to forget and press on. Let go of yesterday so you can fully grasp what God has for you today! —SF

Day 62

———

I Submit to God's Will

Then Moses took his wife and his sons
and set them on a donkey,
and he returned to the land of Egypt.
And Moses took the rod of God in his hand.

Exodus 4:20 (NKJV)

I grew up like a nomad visiting different military bases every few years, but my husband has been waiting 25 years to return to where he grew up. In today's scripture, Moses left his homeland, matured, married, and grew his family before God called him to return to Egypt. I see a lot of Moses in my husband. But today, I'm not looking at Moses and how he obediently heard the Lord and returned. I'm looking to Moses' wife, Zipporah, a foreigner to her husband's homeland.

The Lord called us to loosen our ties from the only home my sons knew and the longest home I've ever had. Let's say that this city has become the homeland I'd return to, if given a chance. In the midst of this new journey, and through tear-soaked cheeks, I sought the Lord.

See, Moses' wife is set upon a donkey and led to a new foreign land. My mind wonders, what in the world was she thinking on that donkey ride? Did she throw a chair when Moses said, "Hey, God told us to move"? I may or may not have done that. Did she ridicule, complain, contradict, scream, yell, cry, or discourage and belittle Moses before leaving, or even on the ride there? Look back at today's verse. What's the answer?

No. We're left wondering because her emotions are not in the Word. When something's not in the Word, I am encouraged by what is IN the Word. Moses' wife got on that donkey, let faith overcome her possible fear and followed where God was calling her. Moses wasn't the only one called to a foreign land, Zipporah was too.

Where is God calling you today? The Lord called me to a land I would never have chosen to live. But because I followed where my husband was led, my marriage is stronger and my family relationships are closer. — DM

Day 63

I Am Called

Faithful is He who calls you,
and He also will bring it to pass.

1 Thessalonians 5:24 (NASB)

One thing I really love about God is that He has complete faith in His ability in us. He isn't the least bit concerned that we won't be able to do all that He has in His heart for us. In fact, if you look at His dealings with Moses in Exodus 3, He gets downright perturbed when His power is doubted because of our inabilities. When God called Moses to lead His people out of Egypt, Moses started listing all the "good" reasons that he couldn't possibly be able to do the task at hand. In the natural, Moses was right. He was a poor speaker and wasn't sure of himself. But God saw beyond the natural. Many times we have the same conversation with God, trying to explain to Him why we aren't able to do what He has called us to do. But God knows something we don't! He knows that His ability in us is greater than any weakness we might struggle with, and He wants us to trust Him to do what He says in spite of ourselves.

As we turn our gaze from our inadequacies to His complete perfection in power and love, we find ourselves doing the impossible to the glory of God. Don't be afraid to let go of your past or your lack of ability. He doesn't take any of that into consideration when He calls you to do something for Him. God wants to give you a dream and purpose so large, you can't possibly fulfill it. Then He wants to do it through you. Try less, trust more.

What is God stirring in your heart that you have laid aside because you thought it was too hard or that you were inadequate to do? Cast that on to Him and let Him do it through you today!
—SF

Day 64

I Am A Beholder

But we all, with unveiled face,
beholding as in a mirror the glory of the Lord,
are being transformed into the same image
from glory to glory,
just as from the Lord, the Spirit.

2 Corinthians 3:18 (NASB)

One Sunday while in my parent's church as a college student, I was seated in the pew and patiently waiting for the service to start. A friend of my parents came in with a visitor and sat a few rows in front of me. As I listened to their conversation, I heard the family friend explain what was going to happen in the service and other odds and ends about the church. I contemplated my responsibility as a believer in that situation and decided I needed to sit up straight and smile as needed, and just try and project as much "Jesus-y" behavior as I could muster. It was in the middle of my "Christian act" when God spoke to my heart and said, "People don't need to see you being Jesus, they just need to see Jesus." Do you ever have those moments where He just gets right to the core of the issue? Whew! Powerful and painful at the same time!

God wants all of us to allow the image of His Son to shine through us. That only happens as we spend time with Him daily and let Him transform us into His image. It isn't going to change anyone else if they see us "acting" like Jesus. But they will forever be changed if we let them see the real Jesus Whom we know and love in our lives.

Honestly, I don't remember what the sermon was about that morning, I just remember the sting of correction and the wondrous work of the Holy Spirit to humble my silly prideful attitude.

Choose today to let Jesus shine through you! —SF

Day 65

I Please God

For we are to God the pleasing aroma of Christ
among those who are being saved
and those who are perishing.

2 Corinthians 2:15 (NIV)

Do you ever think that you please God? You do. You, my beautiful friend, were designed with a purpose—something that only you can do. Just like your fingerprints and your DNA are unique to you, your purpose was designed specifically for you by your Creator. For example, one of my purposes is to help bring to light the beautiful intricacies in the Word of God so you can understand how loved by your Heavenly Father you are.

When we step into our purpose, we feel our Heavenly Father's pleasure.

"I believe that God made me for a purpose. But He also made me fast, and when I run, I feel His pleasure." - Eric Liddell (Chariots of Fire)[3]

What are you created for? What were you designed to do? What is your purpose? That can be a hard one to answer, but a necessary one to explore. A great way to discover your purpose is to ask yourself questions. Great questions produce great answers.

- What did you most love to do at 5 years old? Be specific. What did you love about it?
- What did you most love to do at 12 years old? What did you love about it?
- What do you most love to do now? This is something you can do for long periods without getting bored. It doesn't feel like work.
- What do you do or have done that produces the highest ratio of abundance and satisfaction?

Take some time to pray and then explore these questions. As you dig in, you'll discover what you were created to do. Remember, as you walk in your purpose, you'll feel your Heavenly Father's pleasure.

For Reflection: Attempt to fill in the blank of Liddell's quote for yourself: When I _____, I feel God's pleasure. —HB

Day 66

I Am Right On Track

Let us therefore, as many as are perfect, have this attitude; and if in anything you have a different attitude, God will reveal that also to you; however, let us keep living by that same standard to which we have attained.

Phil 3:15-16 (NASB)

It is such a release when we understand and believe that our growth in Jesus is directed by Someone else. Many times we bury ourselves under expectations and growth-mile-markers that we think are important, but just add extra stress to our lives.

When we take our babies to the pediatricians, they take measurements of their head circumference, their weight, their length, and ask questions about any new learned behaviors. If our babies are consistently falling behind in these areas, there is even a medical term: "failure to thrive." We can take this mentality into our spiritual lives as well, comparing ourselves with other mature believers we respect. If we don't "measure up" in some way, we condemn ourselves or try to defend ourselves to others. In Philippians 3, Paul is encouraging us to let that bad habit go. God knows so much more than us! He sees what skills and habits we are going to need in the future. He knows which things are the most important for us to grow in right now, so that we are ready for what He is going to do through us and for us. We can trust His goodness and faithfulness to hold us by the hand and lead us to victory in all of these areas.

God loves us. If we are going in the wrong direction in any of our attitudes, He WILL correct us. He wants us to be blessed and cooperate with His plans to bless us and others.

Give control of your attitudes and the direction of your life over to God right now. He wants to lead you and help you! —SF

Day 67

I Am A Treasure Vessel

But we have this treasure in earthen vessels,
so that the surpassing greatness of the power
will be of God and not from ourselves;

2 Corinthians 4:7 (NASB)

God is not looking to our perfection or appearance to determine whether He can use us or not. Isn't that a comforting thought? As a stay-at-home mother of four, I am not very impressive on paper. My resume of the last 24 years would be very short, containing references to carpooling, trips to the grocery store, mountains of laundry, and LOTS of dishes! When I attend business functions with my husband, everyone has such interesting topics of conversation and lives of such significance. It is a temptation to believe that my job doesn't matter, and I used to feel intimidated and afraid to speak up about what I thought was a boring life. But God didn't take any of that into account when He called me to teach His Word through speaking and print. Actually, I think He rather likes it. The more broken and humble we are, the more His glory can shine through us as we submit to Him.

I am always amazed when I let the love of God flow through me to other women and professionals I come in contact with—how they are drawn to the love of God living and thriving in my heart. People are drawn to Jesus and authentic Christianity, and as we allow Him to lead us, we will be amazed at what His glory can do through our earthen vessels! He wants to shine His love and light through us if we will just stop discounting ourselves!

Right now, let's let go of the desire to be perfect before God is able to do anything with us. Let's submit to His grace working in us and through us and let Him glorify Himself in our lives! —SF

I Am Living Sent

Also I heard the voice of the Lord, saying:
"Whom shall I send, And who will go for us?"
Then I said, "Here am I! Send me."

Isaiah 6:8 (NKJV)

When the Lord sends you, He opens the way, orders the plans, and instructs the process, and always for a reason!

There is something about crossing the Oklahoma/Missouri state line that brings me a sort of comfort and relief. Ahhh, I'm back to the place I've called home for the last ten years. The air is fresher, the grass is greener, the river is fuller, and the trees are higher. My second son was born here and my oldest son grew up here. In maturity, I grew here relying on my church, mentors, jobs, and friends as sources of knowledge. But I bet you're wondering which side of the state line I'm referring to? When you live sent, you find comfort in the Lord on either side of the line.

Living sent means I am in the hands of the Lord. Jeremiah 26:14 says it perfectly: "As for me, here I am, in your hand; do with me as seems good and proper to you." Wherever He would have me go, there is a purpose for me being there. Whether it's a new job, a new Bible study, a new group of friends, or a whole new state, or even a whole new country.

When we know the Lord is with us and we trust in Him, following His lead to where He is sending us becomes less of a struggle and more of an opportunity. This opportunity brings us closer to our Lord as we lean on Him for strength, leadership, wisdom, and comfort.

Has the Lord burdened you with a glorious purpose you feel you were not ready for? Good thing we are called to rely on the Lord and not on our feelings! What if right now, you viewed this new thing the Lord has called you to do with fresh eyes. The Lord has sent you to where you are with a purpose. Let's receive this purpose from the Lord and say aloud, "Here am I!" — DM

Day 69

I Give What I Have

*"There is a lad here who has five barley loaves
and two fish, but what are these
for so many people?"*

John 6:9 (NASB)

Have you ever had this conversation with God? "Lord, I would love to help my neighbors out with their financial situation, but I just don't have any extra to give." Or maybe, "How can I give to those missionaries in Costa Rica? I need my money to pay for my kids' braces!" God presents us with opportunities to give into His kingdom every day and honestly, our hearts want to give. We were designed by God to want to obey Him and be the image of His generosity here on this earth! But sometimes our pragmatism, or "common sense," gets in the way and overrides our spirit's cries to share God's love.

God's economy is completely different than what we are used to. Common sense says, "A penny saved is a penny earned." But God says, "A penny given to Me is a penny multiplied back to you!" Sometimes we may think that God can only use large amounts of money, or food, or clothes, or time. We need to change our metrics to match God's. He sees the little things. He sees the moments we spend loving others when we are in a hurry or have needs of our own that need to be filled, and honestly that can mean more to Him than the $100 we haphazardly placed in the offering plate last week. With God, it's all about the heart. A small amount given to God out of our love and obedience is priceless to Him.

God doesn't need a million dollars from us to do something through us. He doesn't need $1,000. He doesn't even need $100. He can use two pennies, right? But what God can't do is multiply by 0 and get anything other than 0. God can't multiply what we don't give to Him. We need to turn our eyes from what is in our hands to Him who holds us in His hands.

Read John 6:9-13 now and meditate on what in your life is a loaf and fish—something you could willingly present to the Father to use. As He begins to multiply back to you, write it down in a journal or diary so that you won't forget His faithfulness! It will help you let go faster and easier the next time. —SF

I Am Equipped to Be a Great Mom

Train up a child in the way he should go,
Even when he is old he will not depart from it.

Proverbs 22:6 (NASB)

My husband, two sons, and I enjoy watching the birds in our backyard. Various little and large birds make their way through and around the grass, looking for their tasty treats. Over the years, we have watched many birds bring their newly-flying offspring to our yard. We think it's because we have a "safe" backyard—the only one of its kind in our neighborhood without a dog or cat ready to pounce on them. We have watched baby birds flapping furiously to gain the strength to fly, all the while the mom or pop waited patiently on the wooden fence. They had nothing to worry about when their child landed directly on the ground.

What the birds don't know though is the hidden danger of the many snakes we have in our yard. Countless snakes have roamed through the high grass and bushes, under planter-pots, around old sticks, and even inside our house! Gasp! We know about this danger because we have dealt with it. The birds do not. They are only focused on training.

When it comes to hidden or in-plain-sight danger, we are given the gift of guiding our children. Whether the birds use our "safe-haven" backyard or the dog-patrolled backyard, they are raising their children the best way they know. When things happen in life, we model for our children how to handle situations. Who do we turn to for answers?

My best friend, Sharon, has always said, "Without God, there's no way I could be a good parent! I do my best, and God does the rest!"

Now, ask the Lord for forgiveness for trying to parent without Him. It's been a struggle, right? We were never created to parent alone! Now, thank the Lord for strengthening, guiding, and giving you all you need to raise the gift the Lord blessed you with!! —DM

I Am Strong In Him

And He has said to me,
"My grace is sufficient for you,
for power is perfected in weakness."
Most gladly, therefore, I will rather boast
about my weaknesses,
so that the power of Christ may dwell in me.

2 Corinthians 12:9 (NASB)

I believe someone who knows how weak, inept, and incapable they are within themselves—and falls down at Jesus' feet for mercy and help in time of need—is more effective as a leader and a believer than someone who believes they have it all together and knows just what to do.

As we read scripture, our attitude should be, "I can't do this, but YOU can!"—fully leaning and trusting in HIS ability in us to fulfill His desires for us, in us, and through us. Our job is simply to agree with Him and submit to His work in us, expecting His power to find its completion, purpose, and perfection in our weaknesses.

God isn't looking for people who know what to do for Him, He is looking for people who realize they don't know what to do, and will rely completely on His grace and love for them to accomplish His will. He gives us great things to do not so that we will do great things for Him, but so that we will allow Him to do great things through us. We get to know His goodness and faithfulness better, and He gets to be glorified through our lives as we reflect His will.

Submit your greatest weakness and your greatest strength to God today. Let Him magnify Himself and His grace in your weakness and let Him multiply your strengths as you acknowledge that they came from Him in the first place. —SF?

I Am Safe

"My sheep hear My voice,
and I know them, and they follow Me;
and I give eternal life to them, and they will never perish;
and no one will snatch them out of My hand.
My Father, who has given them to Me, is greater than all;
and no one is able to snatch them
out of the Father's hand."

John 10:27-29 (NASB)

There are times in our lives when our circumstances look rough; they can look downright terrible. I remember one particularly awful week where we had sick kids, overdue bills, broken appliances, and my husband was out of town on a mission trip! I was feeling pretty lousy and kind of angry at God for all the trouble.

All of these circumstances, and even tougher ones such as a death in the family, can lead us to believe that God is distant from us or doesn't care about what is going on in our lives. When we look at God through the lens of our situations, He can look distorted or even evil and cruel. Jesus knew this tendency of sinful humanity, to see things through a broken lens, so He gave His words of truth to hold on to when our situations don't look so good. We should look to God's Word to tell us the truth, not our situations or our experiences. They will change. God's Word will not!

You don't have to get upset when someone treats you poorly or unfairly. Their choices aren't about you anyway. When things break in this broken world, you can rest in something greater. You are so incredibly loved, safe, and secure in the Father's heart, there is nothing that can steal that or diminish it in any way. God loves you! Everything else is gravy! Choose today to believe and proclaim what He says, even if it doesn't match what you see.
—SF

I Am Chosen

The poor and needy seek water,
but there is none, their tongues fail for thirst.
I, the Lord, will hear them;
I, the God of Israel, will not forsake them.

Isaiah 41:17 (NKJV)

Bakeries are one of my favorite places to enjoy a cup of coffee and a sweet treat. There is a warm, inviting smell that leads you to the glass cases of homemade goodies. Choosing one is difficult, as I'd rather have them all! One thing I have noticed at my favorite bakeries is that there are always more than one option. Those wonderful delectable items are nestled near other delectable items. And the baker stands ready to hand over his handcrafted work for your enjoyment.

And then there is always an area where some items are reduced in price because they lost their potency and flavor after a few days. No one chose them to be their treat. This is not the case with our Father! Each day, we are like freshly baked, hand-crafted items that are always chosen. We are hand-picked and wanted by our Savior. There is no question on when we'll be chosen because we always will.

Right now, there may be a situation you are in where you feel like day-old sweet treats. Let me tell you that you have not been forgotten, forsaken, passed over, or left behind. The Lord sees you and hears you. Each and every word.

Find a few minutes to close this devotional for today and pray out loud. Thank your heavenly Father for never leaving you and for always choosing you. You are His Beloved!! Thank Him for hearing you and seeing your face. The Lord and Savior has never left you, nor will He! —DM

Day 74

I Am Usable

He spat on the ground, and made clay of the spittle,
and applied the clay to his eyes, and said to him,
"Go, wash in the pool of Siloam"
(which is translated, Sent).
So he went away and washed, and came back seeing.

John 9:6-7 (NASB)

There was a patch of clay on the ground near Siloam, that was trampled on every single day. It looked just like all the other earth surrounding it. When it rained, little kids squished it between their toes. Adults washed it off their feet when they got to their destination. It was really not special in any sense. It wasn't a precious jewel and it didn't contain any gold dust. It didn't even get formed into a pot for use in the kitchen or a bathroom! But when God saw that patch of clay, He didn't see dirt. He saw new eyes!

I once worked in the Ophthalmology Department at a world renowned Medical Center, and I can tell you that the eyeball is incredibly complex and requires great care to work properly. There are micro-vessels supplying the fragile cells throughout, and it even has its own immune system to keep inflammation from damaging our vision. It is truly an illustration of God's care and creativity!

When you feel like dust, powdered earth, broken clay, in pieces on the ground, with no form or reason for being… remember that God sees who you really are. He sees your potential in His Hands. Trust Him. He used discarded clay to make the mud that opened the eyes of the blind. We may feel like dirt, but in the Hands of the Father, we are eyes for the blind! —SF

Day 75

I Am New

Therefore if anyone is in Christ,
he is a new creature;
the old things passed away; behold,
new things have come.

2 Corinthians 5:17 (NASB)

I took a personality test during my youth that was designed to tell me more about myself. It was based on my natural disposition and temperament, and sought to inform me about what I was strong at and what I was weak at. This information was in turn supposed to help me become a better person, or at least not be surprised by the areas that caused me to stumble.

As I grew in my knowledge of God's Word, He began to challenge those assertions about who I was. I had allowed this test to identify me as lazy, so doing what I needed to get done every day was a struggle. I had believed this report that I was an extrovert, so I was insecure when alone. God began to show me that who I am in the flesh is broken, but who I am in Christ is complete and doesn't struggle with those things. Jesus conquered them for me!

When we find our identity in anything other than God's Word, we are hindering the fullness of Christ in our lives, and limiting what He wants to do through us and for us.

What are some negative personality traits you have adopted as your own, such as "I'm lazy", "I'm not organized", "I'm not patient", or "I'm not a leader"? Find some scriptures today that directly speak to those natural tendencies and answer them with His power and grace for you. Now, speak God's words over yourself and believe them about yourself. That's who God has made you in Christ! As you grow in your knowledge of God, you will mature into your big brother Jesus! —SF

I Am A Spring-maker

How blessed is the man whose strength is in You,
In whose heart are the highways to Zion!
Passing through the valley of Baca they make it a spring;
The early rain also covers it with blessings.

Psalm 84:5-6 (NASB)

Everyone goes through challenging seasons in life. That's just the way things on this broken ball of earth go. Even Jesus had his moments of temptation in the desert, going hungry and thirsty and facing the devil at every turn!

But when we find our identity and our belief system in God's Word, it will change who we are and what we do. When we understand that our strength is found in God, we find our strength inexhaustible. When our heart is on the path to His kingdom, we find we are never lost again. We don't allow the outside forces of negativity to enter into our hearts. We rest, knowing He has us in the palm of His Hand and we couldn't be safer.

But that's not all! Take a look at how this person changes the environment around them in the verse here: Passing through (not stopping and making a camp) the valley of Baca (a season of hardship, literally means "weeping" or "sorrow") they make it a spring (It becomes a source of refreshment for themselves and those following after them!) The early rain also covers it with blessings (God rushes to meet this person with His goodness!)

This is who you are in Christ! As you find your strength in Him, and you submit to His direction for your life, this is your new identity. Meditate on this word today and confess it specifically about your situation. You are a Spring-maker in the midst of challenges and trials! —SF

Day 77

I Am Not Alone

Be strong and courageous.
Do not be afraid or terrified because of them,
for the Lord your God goes with you;
he will never leave you nor forsake you.

Deuteronomy 31:6 (NIV)

The Lord says right here in His word that He is with us. He will never leave us. What shall we have to fear if our Protector is always with us? Sleep has not always been a friend of mine. For years, my husband would be gone sporadically for 6 months out of the year. Fear crept in and took hold of my thought life. Worries would plague me each and every night. Like a young fearful child, I would sleep with all the lights on. My younger sons would wake up and ask for the lights to be turned off. They had no fear! They wanted to sleep!

I had believed the lie that when my husband was gone, I was alone. That is simply not true!! The Lord is always with us! Maybe we have been abandoned or deserted by those who said they would never forsake us. Our Father has many names, but abandoner and deserter are not some of them. He's there every second, of every hour, of every day, of every week, of every month, of every year, and so on. He doesn't go away when you're mad at Him or when you do something wrong. He doesn't forget your birthday or forget how precious you are. He is our Father who art in heaven, our shepherd, our righteousness, our banner, our provider, our healer, our peace, and our Lord Who is present—all the time!

Wanting to resist the lie that I was alone, I began confessing the Word of the Lord, especially Psalm 4:8. I began visualizing angels around me. I sang one of my favorite songs, and listened to worship music before going to sleep. I would wake up refreshed and comforted by the One who is always with me, my Lord!

Right now, this very moment, the Lord is with you. If you're reading this during the day or alone at night seeking comfort, you are not alone. Be strong and courageous and call on the Lord for He has never left you.—DM

Day 78

I Have Confidence and Value

But blessed is the one who trusts in the Lord,
whose confidence is in him.

Jeremiah 17:7 (NIV)

Following an afternoon of doctor's appointments with my son, we were famished. He chose a sandwich shop, and I chose a new adventure. I heard from my small group about this great new chicken salad eatery. Walking in, we were greeted by lovely, smiling faces. But while eating, I noticed these lovely, smiling faces turned grim upon the arrival of what must be their manager. While sitting in the eatery, his voice of ridicule and contempt sucked the air dry of joy. The Lord showed me the eyes of the ladies—they needed love. But being lowly, housewife, void-of-a-business-degree "me", what could I do?

The Lord calls us to pray to Him. About anything. That's right. He doesn't say, "okay, pray about this, but not this." Or, "that's a weird prayer, but okay." He says in His word to pray without ceasing. Pray about anything. Lean on His strength and understanding.

So what did I do? I prayed for an opening for what God was calling me to do. "Lord, You know what You would have me do." I sat for another minute quietly hearing the Lord. (Yes, this was a time when my 9 year old boy was quiet, abnormally quiet! Had to be Jesus!)

The owner of the store, an elderly man, walked in and walked directly to our table. He didn't stop to say hello to others, he came right to us. After questioning our enjoyment, I mentioned that I had a concern with the manager's treatment of women. He spent almost an hour with us. When leaving, he couldn't thank me enough for hearing the Lord (he was a believer, too!) and sharing with him when others would have only hid behind a review on social media.

Resist the lie that you have no value! You have confidence in the Lord and when you don't have the answers, that's okay!! Our Lord does! Take a minute right now to call on the Lord to fill you with the confidence to walk in God's Best for your life! — DM

Day 79

I Am Restored in Christ

The Spirit of the Lord God is upon me,
Because the Lord has anointed me
To bring good news to the afflicted;
He has sent me to bind up the brokenhearted,
To proclaim liberty to captives
And freedom to prisoners;
To proclaim the favorable year of the Lord
And the day of vengeance of our God;
To comfort all who mourn,
To grant those who mourn in Zion,
Giving them a garland instead of ashes,
The oil of gladness instead of mourning,
The mantle of praise instead of a spirit of fainting.
So they will be called oaks of righteousness,
The planting of the Lord, that He may be glorified.

Isaiah 61:1-3 (NASB)

In September of 2017, My husband and I took a wonderful trip to Ireland to mark our 25th wedding anniversary. We had just witnessed the wedding of our eldest child to a lovely young lady, and it was a momentous trip for us to say the least. Below is what I wrote about it in my journal. I believe it will bless you, because God is no respecter of persons—which means if He did it for me, He will do it for you!

"Over the last 25 years, Greg Fletcher and I have made many memories. To actually get to this landmark was a lot of hard work for us. We both came to our marriage with many broken areas in our lives and as we started our new life together, it was clear to both of us that we were going to need the grace of God to succeed. He was always so faithful to meet us where we were, and help us when we asked, but we still had to put into practice the lessons He gave us.

This Ireland trip is a testimony for us—a testimony that if you trust God, obey His Word, and do the hard things, He can turn even your broken humanness into something beautiful. There were many times in our 25 years that all we had left after a fight was ashes. When we gave those ashes to Him, instead of throwing them away, He gave us His beauty. He is SO GOOD and wants to do that for you too!"

To take the broken things in our lives and restore them is His specialty! He loves us so! He wants to give you beauty for ashes, gladness instead of mourning, praise in place of fainting, and His righteousness for our filthy rags. All of these things give Him glory and He loves doing it! Give Him your broken heart, your broken dreams, your broken marriage, your broken friendships, your broken body, and your broken life today. —SF

Day 80

———

I Trust in the Lord

*May the God of hope fill you with all joy and peace
as you trust in him, so that you may overflow
with hope by the power of the Holy Spirit.*

Romans 15:13 (NIV)

While watching a group "trust" exercise—you know the one, where you have to fall back on people you barely know and expect them to catch you—a thought hit me. This exercise has never been easy for me because, let's face it, I do not trust people I barely know. Falling back and hoping they catch me is much different than trusting them to catch me. Now, would this be easier with my trusted best friends? Of course! I've spent years living life with them, walking through victories and struggles, and worshiping the Lord together.

Do you trust the Lord? Does falling back into His arms seem like a trust-fall exercise gone wrong, ending with you hitting the floor? I realized that the ones I trust the most are the ones I know the most. Spending time in God's Word brings me into a more intimate relationship with my Father. I trust Him when I have spent time with Him. I know Him and walked through victories—victories such as His incredible Son, have you met Him? He's pretty trustworthy. The situation that Jesus' mother had while being pregnant and betrothed but not married, was God's way of sending His Son to save us all. What looked like a tragedy in the making turned into a victory in the end. These stories show the infinite love our Father has for us. He shows the joy and peace we have when we trust Him.

Right now, you may have something you are trusting the Lord to do, to take care of, to walk you through, or to answer. Falling back into the Lord's arms —the most powerful trust fall of your life— will bring peace and joy. You've heard "Let go and let God," and now is the time to do exactly that! Pray to your Savior, open the Bible, and seek out who He is and why you can trust Him with everything! — DM

Day 81

———

I Am A Usable Vessel

"Then the kingdom of heaven will be comparable to ten virgins, who took their lamps and went out to meet the bridegroom. Five of them were foolish, and five were prudent. For when the foolish took their lamps, they took no oil with them, but the prudent took oil in flasks along with their lamps. Now while the bridegroom was delaying, they all got drowsy and began to sleep. But at midnight there was a shout, 'Behold, the bridegroom! Come out to meet him.' Then all those virgins rose and trimmed their lamps. The foolish said to the prudent, 'Give us some of your oil, for our lamps are going out.' But the prudent answered, 'No, there will not be enough for us and you too; go instead to the dealers and buy some for yourselves.' And while they were going away to make the purchase, the bridegroom came, and those who were ready went in with him to the wedding feast; and the door was shut. Later the other virgins also came, saying, 'Lord, lord, open up for us.' But he answered, 'Truly I say to you, I do not know you.' Be on the alert then, for you do not know the day nor the hour.

Matthew 25:1-13 (NASB)

Let's meditate on the parable of the ten virgins today, found in Matthew 25:1-13. It has confused me to some degree because I thought it was talking about the final wedding feast of the Lamb and it seemed like some Christians were going to be left out. I think, perhaps, it is addressing the moves of God in the earth today. There are certain works God is doing all around us that we can be a part of, if we will prepare our lamps—our hearts—and get the oil of the Holy Spirit's Presence—His anointing—by spending time with Him. He wants us to be usable and to be a blessing to those people around us. But we also have a part to play. There is a difference between being righteous because of Christ, and being usable through sanctification. Being sanctified means allowing the Holy Spirit to engage with your humanness and changing as He lovingly convicts us of our errors.

God has given us His righteousness so that we can boldly receive His grace for every purpose and plan He has for us. But there is a cost to our flesh—we are containers of the Holy Spirit because we are called to do hard things, things we don't always find comfortable or fun. If we aren't willing to pay that price, we can't expect God to find us usable. And we certainly shouldn't try leaning on our brothers and sisters in Christ to supply us with what we have every ability to get on our own.

Commit today to do the hard things and fill your oil lamp with the Presence and wisdom of God by spending time with Him and obeying Him. You won't regret it, and you will shine like the stars at night! —SF

Day 82

I Am Never Alone

Now from the sixth hour
darkness fell upon all the land
until the ninth hour.
About the ninth hour
Jesus cried out with a loud voice, saying,
"Eli, Eli, lama sabachthani?" that is,
"My God, My God, why have You forsaken Me?"

Matthew 27:45-46 (NASB)

When Adam and Eve sinned in the Garden of Eden, they were forced to leave the presence of God. Sin in humanity limited God's presence from then on, until the birth of the sinless Son of God, Jesus. Jesus was the first man, since Adam and Eve, to fully enjoy and remain in the presence of His Father constantly. The reason this fact is so important is because we need to know what Jesus purchased for us by giving up His life on the cross. You see, when Jesus was forsaken by God, He did it on purpose. He bore all of our sin and separation from God so that we would never have to again. He proclaimed this separation in Matthew 27.

We have all felt alone, forsaken, and unloved by our God. We have all felt the overwhelming darkness of separation from the only life-giving God of the universe. But because Jesus suffered this on the cross in our place, we don't ever have to be in that place again in our lives. Ever.

Jesus was forsaken by God in our place, so we would never have to be. If you feel alone, forsaken, unloved by God right now, it isn't the truth. Sometimes our feelings lie to us. Reach out to Him. You will find Him there, having been with you the whole time.—SF

Day 83

———————

I Know My Father's Nature

*"And He is the radiance of His glory
and the exact representation of His nature,
and upholds all things by the word of His power."*

Hebrews 1:3 (NASB)

It is dangerous for us to use our experiences or the experiences of others as a measure of what God is like. He isn't actually in control of every facet of your life. He has given you and others the power of choice, and sometimes those choices negatively affect others. He gave control of this earth to Adam and Eve, and they gave it over to Satan when they obeyed him in the Garden of Eden. Those are two of the many reasons our circumstances don't always line up with God's will on this earth.

One of the most destructive habits I see Christians doing in their lives is elevating experience over God's Word. Some believers will even say that their experiences reveal God's will to them, or show them God's character.

If we really want to know what God is like, we have no further to look than the Gospels. The books of Matthew, Mark, Luke, and John were written within 50-75 years of Jesus' life, death, and resurrection. They portray an accurate description of what He was like here on the earth, and are amazingly filled with agreement that is obviously Divinely inspired. The Holy Spirit tells us in Hebrews that Jesus was the exact representation of the Father's nature. As Jesus never condemned the sinner, the Father never condemns the sinner. As Jesus loves the prostitute and the tax collector, the Father loves them. As Jesus went about healing all who were oppressed of the devil, that is God's will as well. Let's all remember that revealing God to us was the reason Jesus came, and let's believe His testimony about God's character today!
—SF

Day 84

I Can Sing to the Lord!

Make a joyful shout to the Lord, all you lands!
Psalms 100:1 (NKJV)

Sing to the Lord, all the earth;
Proclaim the good news
of His salvation from day to day.
1 Chronicles 16:23 (NKJV)

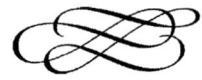

We sing ourselves into His presence making a joyful shout! What is a joyful shout? According to Ephesians 5, it is being "filled with the Spirit, speaking to one another in psalms and hymns and spiritual songs, singing and making melody in your heart to the Lord, giving thanks always for all things to God the Father in the name of our Lord Jesus Christ, submitting to one another in the fear of God."

I have spent time in churches across the nation and am in awe of the spectacular worship to our Father. However, it's never the songs being sung up front or on stage that get me teary-eyed and entering into worship through singing. It's the people around me. The young, the old, the tall, the short, the exquisitely dressed, and the "I-just-woke-up-and-came-to-church" dressed—all these people gathered together in the name of Jesus. Hands up or down, voices loud or soft. We all enter into a joyful shout, a proclamation to the love of our Lord.

Whatever our voice sounds like, we can sing! We can enter into time with the Lord through worship of Him. Off-key, wrong words, soft, loud, however we sing, when we do it unto the glory of the Lord, the Lord is blessed!!! But if you're still wondering about your singing and whether you deem it worthy of worship, take a look at Psalms 95:1, "Oh come, let us sing to the Lord! Let us shout joyfully to the Rock of our salvation." I don't know about you, but when I shout, it doesn't sound like singing. And the Lord says, do that! Shout for Me!

Take a minute right now to free yourself from the idea of perfect singing for worship! Look forward to the next time you get the opportunity to enter into worship with the Lord. He wants to hear your voice of praise and honor! Let your worship be an expression of love between you and the Father and sing a song of praise to Him today! —DM

Day 85

I Am a Receiver

For thus the Lord God, the Holy One of Israel, has said,
"In repentance and rest you will be saved,
In quietness and trust is your strength."
But you were not willing...

Isaiah 30:15 (NASB)

It is completely natural for us as humans to try and earn the favor and love of God and work for what He has promised us. Our lives are full of examples of "work hard to get what you want" and "no pain, no gain." However, this attitude isn't helpful in our spiritual walk with God. The entire purpose of God sending the law through Moses was to show Israel and the world that humanity is incapable of righteousness in its own strength. This fact is designed to drive us to Jesus as our perfect substitute and the fulfillment of the law for us.

Isaiah says here the Jewish state at large wasn't willing to put their trust in God, but instead tried unsuccessfully again and again to fulfill the dictates of the law in the flesh—in their own effort. God's plan was for repentance, rest, quietness, and trust to be their strength, and His plans for us are the same. As we trust in what He has done through Christ, we will find salvation and strength for every area of our lives. It is by His strength and grace all will be accomplished! Doing it in our own strength only produces condemnation when we fail, and pride when we occasionally get it right. Trusting in His grace for us produces thankfulness to God and glorifies His work here on the earth. He gave us Jesus and all that He is, and we have to receive it by faith in Him alone.

It is vitally important for us to remember that all of the promises given to us by God through Jesus Christ are to be received, not achieved. How can you receive His promises today? —SF

Day 86

I Am the Apple of God's Eye

Keep me as the apple of the eye;
Hide me in the shadow of Your wings

Psalm 17:8 (NASB)

I love the idea of being "the apple" of someone's eye. In our culture, it means to be specially selected as a favorite! In the verse here, David uses that phrase when describing his heart toward God's favor on him. He wants to be special and important to the God he loves!

I did further study on this in the Hebrew as it was written, and was so blessed by what I found. I want to share it with you. The literal translation of this phrase "the apple of the eye" is actually not "apple" at all. It is actually saying, "Keep me as the daughter of the eye" and it is referencing our reflection on the eyeball of someone looking at us. You see, when I look at you, your image is reflected on the surface of my eyeball, like a mirror or glass. David is asking God to keep him always in His gaze, as close to Him as David's reflection in God's eyes. He wants God's constant attention!

I have to confess, that image seems so much more tender and intimate with our Father than just a favorite piece of fruit! David's heart of love toward God is also our heart toward our Father today. We love to be with Him, to know we have His complete attention and watchfulness, and to know He cares about every intimate detail of our lives! We were designed by God to want this, and for only His Presence in our lives to satisfy this desire.

Confess to your Loving Father today how much He means to you and ask Him to keep you as the "apple" or "daughter" of His eye. He will do it! —SF

Day 87

I Share God's Presence with Others

As Jesus went on from there,
He saw a man called Matthew,
sitting in the tax collector's booth; and He said to
him, "Follow Me!" And he got up and followed Him.
Then it happened that as Jesus was reclining at
the table in the house, behold, many tax collectors
and sinners came and were dining with Jesus
and His disciples.

Matthew 9:9-10 (NASB)

As Jesus was traveling through Nazareth healing and teaching the people of His hometown, He stopped at the tax collector's booth to talk to the tax collector. In today's world, this would be likened to our stopping to talk to the people working at the DMV counter. Jesus shared the kingdom of God with Matthew, the tax collector, and he became Matthew, the disciple, and immediately followed Jesus right then and there. Tax collectors were an ostracized group of people in the days when Jesus walked on the earth, and were avoided by "polite society." So, it must have been a wonderful feeling for Matthew to be chosen and accepted by this religious teacher so unlike all the Pharisees and Sadducees he had met before.

The immediate effect salvation had on Matthew was that he brought the Presence of Jesus with him as he fellowshipped with his friends that night. He invited Jesus and His other disciples into his dinner party, right at the table with all his tax collector and sinner friends. Funny thing is, they were completely comfortable around Jesus and His disciples and probably had a great time. I am sure Jesus shared the love of God with them, without condemnation. His holiness was never compromised in any way, but I am absolutely certain His Presence changed them all forever. We can't be in His Presence and not be changed. Matthew had done his part in inviting Jesus into every area of his life, and Jesus had graciously accepted. Our response to Jesus is the same today.

Let's invite Him to affect every area of our lives, knowing He is the one that changes those around us. —SF

Day 88

I Am Clothed in Strength and Dignity

Strength and honor are her clothing;
she shall rejoice in time to come.

Proverbs 31:25 (NKJV)

Looking out over the mountains is one of my favorite things to do on vacations. We love the majesty and mystery of the mountains. They are often covered with faint clouds which hide their magnificence. When my husband lived in Seattle, they had what they called a "3-peak" day. That is when the sky is clear and you can see all the mountains in the area. It's astonishingly gorgeous! I enjoyed being there to witness these stellar days. Maybe you noticed something: it's not called "3-peak" week, or "3-peak" month. It's only one day in the middle of the many days of cloudy, dreary rain.

For the believer, we are clothed like the powerful and astounding mountains, but it's not for only a day like in Seattle. We are clothed for the rest of our earthly lives. And it doesn't even stop there! We are clothed in strength and honor for eternity!

Maybe you prefer a beautiful beach sunset or the bright lights of a cityscape over mountains. You may find strength and honor in different views, but one thing always remains in the Proverbs 31 woman. Not only is she clothed in strength and honor, she rejoices in the time to come.

When meditating today on this scripture, remember you are draped in an honor and dignity that only God can give. This strength is fueled by the One who created the universe. If He had the power to create every atom and every molecule, He has the power to give you the strength you pray for! He also gives you a hope for the future—a future that you can rejoice in! — DM

Day 89

I Don't Fear

There is no fear in love;
but perfect love casteth out fear:
because fear hath torment.
He that feareth is not made perfect in love.

1 John 4:18 (KJV)

Fear is such a tricky emotion. It is a feeling and also an action. We may feel uneasy about a situation but still respond in faith and love, or we can actively participate with the emotion and respond with worry and fretting, which only make things worse! With fear, there is always a torment that goes on in the soul and mind, a feeling that everything is NOT going to be okay, or some sense of foreboding evil about to erupt.

I have learned to pay attention to the red flag of torment and ask God to reveal to me where I am in fear somewhere. It is often the case that if I am feeling tormented in my mind in some way, I am believing a lie somewhere. Being "woke" enough to notice this state of torment has helped me tremendously in staying fixed on God's love for me and replace any lies I have believed with the truth of God's Word about my situations.

A great example of this happened a few weeks ago when my husband was growing though a situation with extended family and was having a hard time walking in peace. At first, I responded with anxiety and started snapping back at him, even though I knew I wasn't the source or target of his discomfort. As I prayed, God reminded that fear hath torment, and if I was tormented with thoughts of failure in our marriage or family, I wasn't walking in God's love for me. I realigned my thoughts to agree with His Words and started believing that God was going to work all these things out for our good and that my husband was going to come through it all better than before. I started to agree with God in my heart that my children were blessed, not because Greg or I get it all right, but because of Jesus and His gracious gift of righteousness that we have all received. A wave of peace and joy washed over me. My heart was able to rest in the midst of the stormy weather around me because I was with Jesus.

If you are struggling with torment in any area of your life today, ask God to show you where you are believing fearful thoughts instead of God's love thoughts for you. Now, change your mind!
—SF

Day 90

I Am Filled with Joy

Though you have not seen him, you love him;
and even though you do not see him now,
you believe in him and are filled with an inexpressible
and glorious joy, for you are receiving the end result of
your faith, the salvation of your souls.

1 Peter1:8-9 (NIV)

There is a joy that greatly exceeds the joy culture provides. We have a mockingbird that has taken up claim in our backyard. At first, the beautiful music of his song was neat and interesting. Then, we started to hear his chirping from 6am to 9pm—all day long. His chirping was endless. I thought on how this mockingbird has an inexpressible and glorious joy to share with the world!

We, like our new bird friend, are able to walk through this life with joy that is inexpressible and glorious. When we wake, when we eat, when we take care of kids or other job-related activities, we can worship the Lord joyfully with our actions, words, and our songs.

Being joy-filled doesn't mean we walk in an auto-pilot fashion in our lives, ignoring what is happening around us. We can see what is happening around us, but find our joy in the Lord! When I am filled with joy, the happenings around me do not affect my happiness.

Let's say that we have heard the joy of our mockingbird friend every day for the last two weeks. We have used tactics to encourage him to find a new singing tree post. I'll tell you what though, his joy cannot be deterred. I like to think he is proving to my family how the Lord fills us with wonderful, beautiful joy that circumstances cannot squash.

Take a minute right now and think on the joy of the Lord. Ask the Lord to fill you with joy that others will not understand and will have to ask you about. Then tell them about Jesus and the joy he provides! —DM

I Am a Vessel of Honor

*Nevertheless, the firm foundation of God stands,
having this seal,
"The Lord knows those who are His," and,
"Everyone who names the name of the Lord
is to abstain from wickedness."
Now in a large house there are not only gold and silver
vessels, but also vessels of wood and of earthenware,
and some to honor and some to dishonor.
Therefore, if anyone cleanses himself from these things,
he will be a vessel for honor, sanctified, useful to the
Master, prepared for every good work.*

2 Timothy 2:19-21 (NASB)

There is a misconception within the modern-day church that how a believer is used by God is up to God, and that the Christian bears no responsibility for whether they are used by God or not. Paul addresses this myth in 2 Timothy when he clearly states that we have a part to play to be useful to God.

Vessels in New Testament times were made out of stone, wood, leather, or, most often, clay. The fired pottery could be used for anything from fine dinnerware, to trash cans and toilets, all depending on the quality, beauty, and cleanliness of the vessel. Paul is alluding to this same principle when he tells Timothy to avoid debate and other forms of iniquity because God wants to use him for holy purposes, and filling up his vessel with strife and contention is counter-productive to God's purposes. We would never give our children a drink of cool, clean water out of the mop bucket, would we? Neither would God!

God's purposes for all of our lives are to use us for honorable works that glorify His Name on the earth. He wants to use us to share His love and peace with everyone we meet. God wants to display His good intention through Christ to this lost and dying world. But if we continually engage in things that we know displease and grieve the Holy Spirit, we are mucking up our souls and minds. We won't be a very effective cup to transfer the love of God to the thirsty souls around us. He wants to use us in powerful ways to set people free, but we have to cooperate and let Him clean us up first!

Confess to God right now where you have been letting the world fill your vessel and ask God to clean you up. Commit to staying clean with His help and watch Him use you!—SF

Day 92

I Speak Life

*Being confident of this very thing,
that He who has begun a good work in you
will complete it until the day of Jesus Christ.*

Philippians 1:6 (NKJV)

What do you do when you make a mistake? Do you beat yourself up verbally? Or, do you say, "That's okay, I'll get em' next time"? Negative self-talk keeps us from accomplishing what God's called us to do and be. It is not humility. It is self-defeating. And, others can't be fed by what we bring to the table.

How do we stop the negative self-talk?

Practice Self-Compassion
NO ONE is perfect except Jesus. We don't have to be. That's why Jesus came. We are not the sum of our mistakes.

Stop Talking
Think, "would I say what I'm about to say to myself to my best friend?" The way we talk to ourselves can be a habit. It's time to break it!

Replace Negative Self-Talk
Replace your negative talk with positive talk about yourself. Say something God says about you rather than what you're feeling in the moment. Here's a sample to get you started:

"This always happens to me," becomes "This may have happened to me in the past, but it doesn't have to run my life. I choose to focus on what's going good in my life" (Heb. 12:2; Phil. 4:8).

The words we use today are creating the world we'll experience tomorrow! Never forget, you are treasured and loved by your Heavenly Father! You are gifted and created for such a time as this! Talk to yourself like you are, and create a beautiful opportunity for tomorrow! —HB

Day 93

I Am An Encourager

But encourage one another day after day,
as long as it is still called "Today,"
so that none of you will be hardened
by the deceitfulness of sin.

Hebrews 3:13 (NASB)

In this chapter of the book of Hebrews, the writer is sharing about how unbelief robbed the Israelite nation of the Promised Land for 40 years. Those freed slaves, who had been promised a land flowing with milk and honey, had to settle for merely looking at that land from across the Jordan River because they believed the evil report from their scouting party. The majority report told of the large problems of walls and giants in the Promised Land, but the minority report spoke about God's power and faithfulness and His ability to overcome any obstacle in Israel's way. Unfortunately, the Jews went with the majority report—also called the "evil" report.

There will always be at least two reports over our lives. Which report we give heed to will determine our outcome. We also have the opportunity to choose which scout we will be to the people around us. Do you find yourself saying, "God is faithful, but…." Or do you say, "This trouble is hard, but God is well able to overcome!" Do you hear the difference?

The writer of Hebrews tells us to "encourage one another day after day, as long as it is still called, 'Today.' " He is saying that as long as we are within the confines of time, we have to remind ourselves and each other to focus not on the moment, but on the truth found in God's Word. Once we are free from time, we will be able to see it all and know the final outcome of our time here, but until then, it is shrouded from our understanding. Let's encourage each other to keep pressing forward and not lay claim to what our physical eyes see around us, but instead claim that what our eyes of faith see belongs to us in Christ! This is the good report and finds such favor and pleasure in our Father God! —SF

I Encourage Myself in the Lord

And David was greatly distressed;
for the people spake of stoning him,
because the soul of all the people was grieved,
every man for his sons and for his daughters:
but David encouraged himself in the Lord his God.

1 Samual 30:6 (KJV)

There are seasons in our lives where everything seems to go wrong and it's our fault! This was the situation for David here in 1 Samuel 30. David had just come home after a long military campaign with his men to find his home town burned down and all their wives and children captured by another enemy. All of the soldiers were understandably distraught and became so angry they were even threatening to stone their king over it!

David had a choice to make. It would have been completely natural for him to turn to God in blame. After all, David was out following God's commands at the time, so getting angry with the Lord would make sense. But David really shows us what he is made of here as he instead turns away from man and starts encouraging himself in the Lord his God.

Psalms gives us a great picture of what that looks like over and over as the authors remind themselves of God's faithfulness and power, His loving kindnesses, and His wonderful work in our lives. Remembering God's faithfulness turned things around for David. His despair turned to determination. His anguish turned to adoration. His weeping turned to wisdom, as God answered his cries for help. Ultimately, David and his men retrieved all of their captured families and not one person was lost. They were even rewarded with the spoils of other nations for their troubles! They got back so much more than what was stolen, that David was able to share it all with the best of the nation of Israel!

When you are challenged with negative circumstances today, and are tempted to turn away from God or blame Him for your trials, instead turn to God and remind yourself of Who He is and what He has done for you. Encourage yourself in the Lord, knowing that what He did for David, He will surely do for you too! —SF

I Am Balanced

*For the word of God is living and powerful,
and sharper than any two-edged sword,
piercing even to the division of soul and spirit,
and of joints and marrow, and is a discerner of the
thoughts and intents of the heart.*

Hebrews 4:12 (NKJV)

We recently acquired a lovely pool, but neither my husband nor I have had experience with owning one. The previous owners had not taken care of the pool and it immediately turned green within one week. Unaware of what to do, we went to the closest pool supply store to began treatments. Cleaning the pool took an entire week as the best process was to take care of the pool slowly and not quickly. While waiting, we found "pool school" Youtube videos in order to gain some knowledge about swimming pools. We watched with wide-eyed amazement on the science behind swimming pools—all 14 videos worth!

My favorite thing the instructor said was, "The best pools are the ones where the owners let water do it's thing. It's living and powerful. Just as God made it. God made water to balance out. It's a beautiful thing."

Of course we have to do a little here and there to maintain the right chemicals in order for the pool to be pristine, but the best thing we can do is let the water do its thing. I couldn't help but think about how God's Living Word is the living water Jesus talks about! What a beautiful reminder that God's Word is inherently powerful!

Let's take a minute to reflect on areas of our lives where we may be working to make ourselves balance without the living Word of God. In order to have God's best in our lives, we need to sit back and let God do the work He is doing! Like our now crystal-clear pool, shimmering in the golden sun, we can find ourselves balanced in God's living word. — DM

I Am Clothed in Christ

For you are all sons of God
through faith in Christ Jesus.
For all of you who were baptized
into Christ have clothed yourselves with Christ.

Galatians 3:26-27 (NASB)

I am sure all of us have had a situation of mistaken identity before. One morning a few years ago, I decided to "treat" myself to a grocery shopping trip alone. I say "treat" because at that time we had four kids still at home and I homeschooled them all, so a trip alone to do anything (shower, post office, toilet) was a treat! As I was slowly meandering through the aisles wondering how long I would get to linger and read labels before my oldest called to find out when I would be back, I was startled to feel ten sticky little fingers grab on to my pants leg. I turned my attention from how many ounces were in the jar of spaghetti sauce to the little blond tufted head at my knees. You probably guessed that a little toddler had decided I must be his mom as we were passing each other in the aisle, and as she and I waited for him to realize his mistake we both gave each other the knowing look of mom solidarity. We both knew he would figure it out pretty quickly, and he did and ran right back to his mother while she and I grinned at his cute case of mistaken identity.

This young boy thought my pant leg looked just like his mom's pant leg and treated it as such, until he figured out otherwise! In this same way, God has chosen to clothe us with His Son's identity, so that whenever we come before Him He sees us wearing Jesus' clothes. He purposely put our filthy, moth-eaten, ragged sinfulness on Jesus on the cross, so He could clothe us with Jesus' glorious and holy righteousness from now on. He did that on purpose, because He loves us.

Remind yourself all day today, "I am clothed in Christ today, so God can treat me like He treats Jesus!" —SF

I Glorify God in My Body

Or do you not know that your body
is a temple of the Holy Spirit who is in you,
whom you have from God,
and that you are not your own?
For you have been bought with a price:
therefore glorify God in your body.

1 Corinthians 6:19-20 (NASB)

The Bible confirms for us that we all struggle with sin from time to time, even though we have been redeemed from the curse of it. Often, our mind and soul haven't caught up with the truth of our new birth experience, and we fall into old sin patterns from our former lives. Paul sheds some light on why that happens in 1 Corinthians 6:19-20. He shares these three facts with us that will help us in our struggles with fleshly temptation:

Our body is the temple of the Holy Spirit.
This reminds us that God is always with us to help us and to guide us. We are serving God as we take good care of our health and physical well-being. It is like the priests that used to serve God by caring for His temple in the Old Testament. We don't have arrogant pride about our appearance, but we choose to honor God by caring for the body He gave us to the best of our ability, to His glory.

We are not our own.
Our needs are no longer up to us to meet. When we have physical needs, we can go to the owner of our bodies and ask for help. Any God-given need has its answer with God. He knows what we need, and because we now belong to Him, He wants to meet those needs—all we need to do is ask and trust Him and His timing.

We have been bought with a price.
Our worth is irrevocably tied to the value of Jesus to God, because that's what He paid for us. As we meditate on how much we mean to our Father, the temptations to meet the needs for love and acceptance by sinful means falls away.

As you meditate on these truths today, allow the Lord to show you how this specifically applies to you! He wants to meet your needs! He loves you! —SF

I Have Hope

She senses that her gain is good;
Her lamp does not go out at night.

Proverbs 31:18 (NASB)

Provers 31 is full of rich promises for the Christian woman. I used to believe it was a laundry list of characteristics I had to achieve in order to be qualified as a Godly wife. God has since revealed it to me as a list of character seeds He deposited in my heart at my redemption. Just like all the other blessings in God, they find their beginning and end in Jesus Christ.

As I receive Him as my Lord and Savior, He is the fulfillment of all of God's promises to me. That means my only job is to identify myself with the crucified Christ—my sins were transferred to Him, my iniquities were His at the cross, my weaknesses were crucified with Him in my place. As He received all my failures, I can now receive all His righteousness and wisdom and identity as a citizen of the kingdom of God. That means I am now a Proverbs 31 woman! As I meditate on my new identity, I begin to see myself walking in these wonderful attributes. Because of Christ, I can boldly declare, "I sense that my gain is good, and my lamp does not go out at night!"

That means that God supernaturally reveals to me that my "gain is good," as I receive His fullness in Christ. "Her lamp does not go out at night" means that even though dark times may be upon me and my family, I have a supernatural revelation that God is with me and I know He will work everything out for our good! That is some powerful hope!

God wanted all of these promises listed in Proverbs 31 to belong to you, but you couldn't walk in any of them on your own. So He made a way for you to walk in all of them through Christ. The only thing you have to do to walk in it all is to believe that Jesus paid for it in your place, and receive that it belongs to you now in Christ without any effort to become a Proverbs 31 woman on your own. It's not about you doing it for God, it's about Him doing it through you. He wants the good fruit these characteristics will produce for you in your life just because He loves you! Believe it and receive it today! —SF

I Am His Masterpiece

For we are His workmanship
[His own masterwork, a work of art],
created in Christ Jesus
[reborn from above—spiritually transformed,
renewed, ready to be used] for good works,
which God prepared [for us] beforehand
[taking paths which He set],
so that we would walk in them
[living the good life which He prearranged
and made ready for us].

Ephesians 2:10 (AMP)

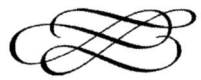

When you read God's Word and you see, "We are His workmanship," how does it make you feel? Do you feel loved and cherished? Or, does your heart feel defeated, like it's not true?

Self-image is defined as the idea, conception, or mental image one has of oneself. How we see ourselves is a vital part of being able to live a fulfilling and prosperous life filled with purpose– the purpose our Heavenly Father put in our heart to fulfill.

Read Ephesians 2:10 again. It's so easy to see ourselves as broken creatures. We're not perfect, but in actuality, we're His masterwork, a work of art. And, because of Jesus, we're spiritually transformed, renewed, ready to be used for good works. He's prearranged a good life for us. We just need to choose to believe that and learn to walk in it.

Will the thing which is formed say to him who formed it, "Why have you made me like this?" Romans 9:20b AMP

You will not change your self-image naturally. You have to purpose to change it. How? Find out your true self through scripture and self-discovery. Then you can see yourself as you truly are.

Start with your Creator: What does He say about you? Study His Word to see. Feel free to look these up in other translations to get a different perspective. Here are a few verses to get you started: Jeremiah 29:11; Ephesians 2:10; 1 Peter 4:10-11; Romans 8:15; 2 Timothy 1:7.

What is your favorite verse(s) that reveals your true self? Write it out on a 3x5 card and read it daily. —HB

Bibliography

1 - C. S. Lewis Quotes." Quotes.net. STANDS4 LLC, 2019. Web. 24 Aug. 2019. <https://www.quotes.net/quote/41227>

2 - ©2016 Billy Graham Evangelistic Association. Used with permission. All rights reserved.

3 - Chariots of Fire Quotes. (n.d.). Quotes.net. Retrieved August 16, 2019, from https://www.quotes.net/mquote/16621.

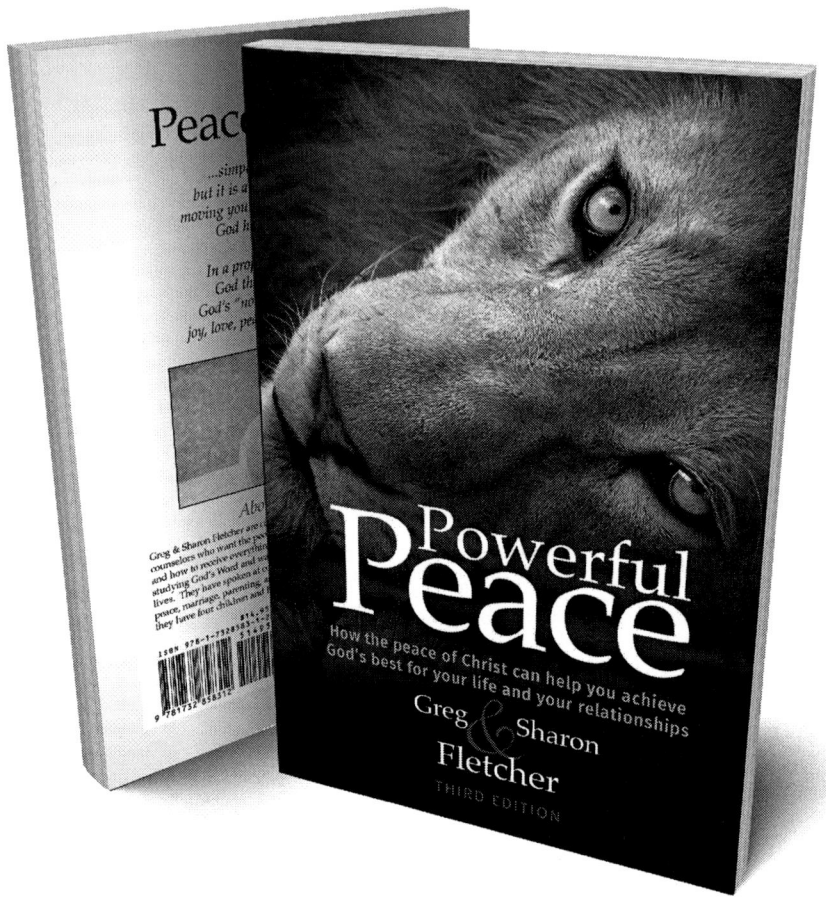

Jesus came to save that which was lost. This includes more than salvation from hell but includes all of what was lost.

This book is for Christians who want a deeper look at Jesus' ministry, crucifixtion and resurrection and how it can impact their every day lives. It will explain and impart a passion for what Jesus accomplished for you and increase the intimacy in your walk with Jesus.

Visit Gods-Best.com for more information

Study Guide for New Believers!

Tools For Living is a friendly study course for new Christians to help them establish great habits and consistency in their new life in Christ!

- An excellent Bible companion that will teach the reader great habits when following Jesus
- A great resouce for church small groups and Bible studies
- 8 weeks of daily Bible readings with personal application
- 4 weeks of doctrinal teaching
- Biblical answers for the new believer's frequently asked questions
- Written in an easy to read and understand style
- Also perfect for youth and for parents to read to their children

Visit Gods-Best.com for more information